THE
AMERICAN
PRESIDENCY

A MILLER CENTER TENTH ANNIVERSARY
COMMEMORATIVE PUBLICATION 1975-1985

THE
AMERICAN
PRESIDENCY

Perspectives
From Abroad

EDITED BY
Kenneth W. Thompson

UNIVERSITY
PRESS OF
AMERICA

Lanham • New York • London

Copyright © 1986 by

University Press of America,® Inc.

4720 Boston Way
Lanham, MD 20706

3 Henrietta Street
London WC2E 8LU England

Library of Congress Cataloging in Publication Data

The American presidency.

"A Miller Center tenth anniversary commemorative
publication 1975-1985."
"Co-published by arrangement with the White Burkett
Miller Center of Public Affairs, University of
Virginia"—Verso of t.p.
Bibliography: p.
1. Presidents—United States. 2. United States—
Foreign opinion. I. Thompson, Kenneth W. II. White
Burkett Miller Center.
JK518.A64 1986 353.03'1 86-13142
ISBN 0-8191-5486-5 (alk. paper)
ISBN 0-8191-5487-3 (pbk. : alk. paper)

The views expressed by the author(s) of this publication do not
necessarily represent the opinions of the Miller Center. We hold to
Jefferson's dictum that: "Truth is the proper and sufficient antagonist
to error, and has nothing to fear from the conflict, unless by human
interposition, disarmed of her natural weapons, free
argument and debate."

Co-published by arrangement with
The White Burkett Miller Center of Public Affairs,
University of Virginia

Dedicated
to the
Memory
of
Professor Hedley Bull
Oxford University
England

PREFACE

From the days of Alexis de Tocqueville and Lord Bryce, the perceptions of non-Americans have added greatly to understanding the American political system. With these contributions in mind, the Miller Center of Public Affairs at the University of Virginia has invited respected observers from abroad to contribute to discussions on the American presidency. Some have visited the University of Virginia, others have submitted papers for discussion and publication.

This Series which is also associated with our Tenth Anniversary opens on a tragic note. Our initial speaker was Professor Hedley Bull who on a visit to Charlottesville viewed the presidency from the perspective of Britain and Australia. Before we could bring the volume to press, Hedley passed away. All who have drawn on his wise and penetrating writings on history and public and international affairs mourn his loss. We dedicate this volume to his memory.

TABLE OF CONTENTS

INTRODUCTION

The contributors to the present volume span the globe and represent the perspectives of observers from Britain, Germany, Austria, Mexico and India. Their reflections on the American presidency provide views from developed and developing countries and from four continents.

Two contributors have for the past three or four decades been leading students of the American scene from Great Britain. Hedley Bull stands in the forefront of students of international relations and his writings will remain a precious legacy of enduring thought on foreign policy and world problems. H.G. Nicholas has written widely on American affairs and his *The Nature of American Politics* from which his essay is excerpted is a small classic of comparative political analysis.

Margarita Mathiopoulos is a young scholar in Bonn, Germany, whose insightful essays on politics, foreign policy and political theory have attracted the attention of Americans writing in comparative government.

Dr. Oliver Rathkolb of the Österreichische Gesellschaft für Zeitgeschichte in Vienna, Austria is a leading authority on American affairs. He has done extensive research and writing in the Kreisky-Archives and served as a consultant to Federal Chancellor Bruno Kreisky.

Francisco Cuevas Cancino is Mexican ambassador to the Court of St. James. He served earlier as Mexican ambassador to the United Nations and UNESCO. Before taking on diplomatic responsibilities for the government of Mexico, he was director of the International Relations program at El Colegio de Mexico in Mexico City. His young collaborator in the present work is Rene Herrera.

Ambassador T.N. Kaul of India is both scholar and diplomat. He joined the Indian Civil Service in 1937 and served until India's independence in 1947. He has represented his country in Moscow, Washington and Peking (Bejing). His scholarship is reflected in the Nehru Memorial Lectures and in such works as *Diplomacy in War and Peace*.

Taken together the individual views of the contributors to this volume add a new dimension of thought on the presidency and public affairs.

CHAPTER 1

THE AMERICAN PRESIDENCY VIEWED FROM BRITAIN AND AUSTRALIA

Hedley Bull

Narrator: Within the year 1985 we embark on a somewhat unique set of activities at the Miller Center, a little different from what we've been doing in recent times. We inaugurate what we hope will be a series of discussions on the American presidency viewed from other countries. If this problem has always been important, its importance has been highlighted in the last several years by some of the seeming differences and misunderstandings that have arisen. The exchange of ideas across bodies of water and national boundaries takes on an importance even greater than in the past. We hope that the discussion will lead to a continuation of exchanges of this kind.

It is altogether appropriate that the first of our discussions, conversations, and exchanges on the American presidency should be with a leading intellectual figure of a country which has given us our legal and political heritage. It stands at the center of the civilization from which the United States emerged. Once Churchill proposed Britain and the United States should rejoin one another and restore their former political unity. England is undoubtedly closer to us than any other country in tradition, language, values, and the heritage of Western civilization.

Hedley Bull is the foremost scholar in Great Britain in the field of international relations. He occupies the major chair at Oxford University. He has written a series of books that have attracted worldwide attention, not least *The Anarchical Society*. He continues to work on the history of the modern state system. Not only has he published his own works of great distinction but, as a labor of love and as an intellectual contribution of high merit, he has edited and brought to publication some unfinished and unpublished writings that the late Martin Wight left behind. He updated a famous Martin Wight book,

1

Power Politics, a classic work in its field, again based on Wight's unpublished notes. We are pleased to invite the ideas, perspectives and impressions of Professor Hedley Bull on the American presidency viewed from Britain and Australia. It is a great privilege to have him with us.

Professor Bull: Thank you. I am very grateful for the opportunity to come here and see the Center about which I have heard a good deal and I look forward to an exchange of views. I shall not speak for very long because I don't think I have a great deal to say: this is not a subject that I have studied in great depth, but of course it is a subject that is so important that everyone who thinks about international affairs is bound to devote some attention to it. I shall speak about the presidency as it is seen from the point of view of the allies of the United States, and more particularly from the points of view of the two countries that I know best—Britain and Australia. These two countries see it to some extent from a similar perspective. They both see it from the point of view of the parliamentary system of government and from the point of view of English-speaking states that, as the chairman said, have a great deal in common with the United States in terms of values. Perhaps they also see it in some respects from the point of view of countries that are of converging importance, one of them a declining great power, the other one a rising small power that has become rather more important.

There are also some differences in their perspectives. The British perspective, these days, has to be seen in the context of Western Europe as a whole; it reflects British membership in the European Economic Community, and the importance that the British government attaches to working in tandem with its Western European allies. There is now something that in the EEC countries is called European political cooperation, a process of foreign policy coordination which requires British governments constantly to cooperate with their counterparts in the other governments of the Community, to try to find common points of view on some of the matters that have already been an issue between Europe and America, like the pipeline issue. This has been one of the dimensions of British policy. Britain's relationship with the United States has to be seen today in the context of Britain's membership in Europe. It has also to be seen, of course, in the context of NATO; Britain relates to the United States within this wider framework.

Australia tends to see the United States in a somewhat more isolated perspective. Australia, of course, is linked with the United States and New Zealand in the Anzus Treaty. It is also a member of the Manila Pact; it is a habitual ally of the United States in the Pacific. But the Anzus system and the Manila Pact system are not the equivalent of NATO. Australia is not a part of some enormous phalanx of powers in that part of the world. It is a small country which feels isolated, which feels possibly expendable from an American point of view, which has a deep anxiety about the possibility of being left on its own and exposed to stronger neighbors, which has an anxiety rooted in memories of the Japanese thrust into the South Pacific in 1942.

Now the President of the United States is a sort of *ex-officio* leader of the West, not merely of NATO and Anzus Treaty and other regional alliances but in a broader sense of the Western combination of states. Though the allies do not play any part in the election of the President of the United States, they nevertheless recognize in the person who holds that office somebody who has a kind of an *ex-officio* position of leadership within the whole of the Western world.

I remember one rather dramatic occasion in which that point was made very well. It was the occasion of the assassination of President Kennedy, when I happened to be in the United States. At that time there was a BBC television program called "That Was the Week That Was," which was a program of political satire. They put on a special edition to mark the assassination, I think on the day of the assassination or the day after. This normally satirical and irreverent program suddenly took on a serious note. The opening words of the program were spoken by Bernard Levin who said, "The President of the United States is the President of Britain." There is a sense in which that is so. The U.S. President, though he is not part of the political apparatus or system of any of the other Western countries, enjoys not only great power in relation to the citizens of Western countries other than the United States (including, because of his authority to order the use of nuclear weapons, the power of life and death over them) but also an ex-officio position of responsibility or knowledge leadership.

This may be marginally less true today than it was twenty years ago, at the time of the assassination of Kennedy. The divisions in the alliance are now somewhat more serious than they were then. I also think that the United States does not loom quite as large within the alliance or within the world now as it did twenty years ago. In the course of that last twenty years American power has declined in the world; militarily, it has declined in relation to the Soviet Union; economically, it has declined in relation to Europe and Japan; and politically, it has suffered a series of defeats and humiliations at the hands of the Third World. And the United States does not walk so tall as it did in the years of President Kennedy, and in particular in the context of the alliance. It is an important change that the United States, when it looks to Europe, perceives an economically very powerful combination of states; the European Economic Community in trading terms is something comparable to the United States, and Japan is also. There is a rough equality in economic terms within the Western alliance that was not there before.

Now this does not mean that the United States has ceased to be the leader of the West. In military terms the United States is certainly still supreme, and also, perhaps more basically, the United States is still a single power. It is able to act politically on the stage of world politics in a way that Europe is not. The unity of Europe is still an aspiration and it's no good saying, as some people do, that if you total up the population of Western Europe and you total up its gross national product and so on, it is bigger than America. That may be true, but Europe does not have the ability that the United States has to act politically, it lacks the political singularity of America. And of course the focus of singularity is the President, the person who can make it act, or can sometimes make it act.

On the whole, American Presidents are well thought of in the alliance. I would, for example, hazard a couple of propositions. One would be that American Presidents in the postwar-period have, by and large, been more popular within the alliance than they have been within the United States, or certainly in the parts of the alliance to which I am especially referring. Franklin Roosevelt, for example, faced a great deal of opposition within America. I remember my surprise on first meeting Americans who hated Franklin Roosevelt, and of course that reflected all the great domestic controversies over Roosevelt's New Deal policies and other matters. But from the point of view of the United Kingdom or Australia, Franklin Roosevelt was the man who brought America into the war on our side, won the war and saved us. It is often the case that political leaders are more popular outside their own countries than they are inside them. It is also true not only of Franklin Roosevelt, but also of subsequent Presidents, although it is less true of President Reagan. President Carter was better thought of outside the United States than inside. I think President Kennedy was perceived as a beacon light in the Western alliance; he was thought to be a great symbol of a revitalized, young America, giving not only a practical but also a moral lead to the West as a whole. The opposition to Kennedy that did extend within America was not much outside the country.

Another proposition I would hazard would be that in the perpetual tussles between the President and Congress, the sympathies of the allies are generally on the side of the President rather than of Congress. We generally think that what the President is trying to do is the right thing, and that he is being obstructed by a Senate or a House of Representatives that has not seen the light. A classic example is the sympathy that existed in the West for President Wilson, when the Versailles Treaty was rejected by the Senate leading to the failure of the United States to enter the League of Nations, and the period of American isolation in the interwar years. President Roosevelt's attempts to shift America away from neutrality and commit it to enter the Second World War, at a time when Congress was basically unfriendly to this course, is another example. President Truman's dismissal of General MacArthur was widely hailed in the alliance, certainly in Britain and in Australia.

At the moment, President Reagan's attempts to get the Congress to provide funds for the International Monetary Fund (IMF) is in this tradition. It is possible, of course, to find contrary examples. In the Vietnam War there was a lot of sympathy in Europe for the congressional assault on President Johnson's conduct of the war, although people in Europe were not by any means unanimous about that. But while there are examples where sympathies have lain more with Congress, more commonly the opinion within the allied countries has tended to be sympathetic to the President.

I want now to mention five sources of difficulty that exist in the alliance, all of which are connected with the presidency. I don't think the character of the presidency is the chief problem in relations between America and its allies but it is one of the problems. The way the Europeans and others perceive the presidency in some ways contributes to the problem of holding the alliance together.

The first difficulty has to do with the differences of political style between European countries and the United States. The President of the United States is an immensely visible person from the moment he is elected. Indeed from the moment he is identified as a possible candidate through the primary elections and his efforts to be adopted as a candidate, he is a wholly visible person. This process of choosing and electing a President, and later his occupancy of the presidency itself, is an immensely public one. It reflects all the character of American political life. The way politics are conducted in the United States is, from a British and European point of view, in some respects alien; America is a very different kind of political society and things are done here in a very different way. There is a public relations element that is central to the American political process, an element of ballyhoo, a folksy element, which, when seen out of context, is strange and even alarming. When an Englishman, for example, switches on television and sees an American party convention, he will often consider it a circus and an absurd way of conducting politics. The back-slapping side of American politics, the grin that is so often on the face of an American President, the subordination of substance to appearance, may be taken to be a sign of lack of maturity or sophistication. But those who live in the United States and see all this in context, realize that it is not irrational but makes sense. The element of ballyhoo is a necessary condition of effective participation in American political life. A party convention is not all dancing girls and balloons but is also a place where serious business is settled. Back-slapping and *bonhomie* may be a sign, not of lack of sophistication, but of awareness of the rules of the political game. The difference in political style between Britain and America reflect the fact that America is a democracy in a deeper sense than is Britain, at least in some senses of the form. It is also a democracy in a deeper sense than Australia, I believe. Australia is, in some respects, a more egalitarian country than America is; it has more economic equality, and a stronger commitment to belief in social equality. But Australia, though a "new" country and a country of immigration, having a lot in common with America in these respects, is ultimately still a monarchy and a colonial country, with a certain deference to authority—much less than in Britain, but more so than in the United States.

A second and more serious source of difficulty is the perplexity that is caused in the minds of people who live in countries like Britain and Australia by the system of separation of powers, the division of powers between the President and Congress. When Walter Bagehot wrote his famous book on *The English Constitution,* people imagined that Britain also had a system of separation of powers, because this was what Montesquieu had said, and indeed there is a separation of powers in the United Kingdom, between the executive and the legislature on the one hand, and the judiciary on the other. But as Bagehot pointed out in his book, the British system, which is also the Australian system, is not based on the separation of powers but the fusion of powers. The executive and the legislature are not in perpetual contest in the way in which they are in the United States because the executive in effect controls the legislature through the party system. The prime minister of the United Kingdom is a person appointed by the queen because he or she is in the position to command a majority of the members of the House of Commons. Because the prime minister is also the leader of the majority party in the House of Commons, he or she nearly always can command a majority in that House; when the prime minister, with the backing of the party, is set on a policy, that policy will be voted through the House of Commons without any need for struggle to ensure its passage. Of course, in the last analysis the House of Commons can dismiss the prime minister, and sometimes this happens. It happened in 1940, for example, when enough Conservatives became dissatisfied with Neville Chamberlain's leadership that he had to go; even without an election he lost the support in the House of Commons necessary to sustain government. But in a normal situation, because of party discipline, the prime minister can expect to get his or her policies endorsed by the legislature.

Now when people in the Allied countries look to the President of the United States they find it difficult to grasp that he is not like the prime minister of Britain or Australia in this respect. The President may enter into understandings with allies, but there is no guarantee that it is the President's policies that will prevail. Whether or not he can deliver the goods depends on the Congress, and sometimes the President is defeated, to the chagrin of the allies. In celebrated instances like the Senate's rejection of the Treaty of Versailles, or perhaps the inability of President Carter to have the Senate ratify the SALT II Treaty—these have been sources of great discontent to America's partners. This is a special difficulty because of the central international position of the United States and because the President is not just the President of the United States, but also the leading figure in the alliance as a whole. He has international responsibilities; he has responsibilities not just to his own people in his own system, but also responsibilities that follow from his being the leading figure in this alliance. But the system does not always allow him to satisfy the expectations that those outside America have of him. He is not in charge of the United States in the way in which the prime ministers of parliamentary government countries are in charge of their countries.

Now there is a third problem, and that is that the President of the United States constantly has to talk to two audiences, a foreign audience and a domestic audience. In this respect the President is not unique; this might be said of all national leaders. They all make some international impact. Their speeches are recorded abroad and they have audiences outside the country who listen to them while they also speak internally. But this is especially difficult in the case of the United States, because what the President of the United States says is so important; it is reported everywhere, studied minutely for all its nuances, and all over the world people are sensitive to what he might say. And yet most of what the

President of the United States says is not directed deliberately towards a foreign audience; it is mostly directed towards a domestic audience inevitably and rightly so because the United States is a democracy. The President of the United States has to concern himself with getting re-elected and with getting the political support in Congress and in the country necessary to carry his policies through. But sometimes the things that it is necessary to say domestically in order to sustain the power base, the domestic position of the President, are unhelpful to the policies of the country abroad. There is not much that can be done about this; it just is the case that there is a contradiction in this respect between the requirements of domestic policy and the requirements of international policy.

Now if I could illustrate in the present phase—not just in the Reagan period, it was true in the Carter period also—the United States, like a lot of other countries in the world at present, is in a nationalist and unilateralist mood. I referred earlier to the decline of the American power and the setbacks received and humiliations suffered by the United States in recent decades, particularly in the 1970s. I believe that as a consequence of that, there is in this country a mood of national reassertion; people in America have had enough of being pushed around and being criticized, suffering setbacks and defeats, and there is a desire in America to assert the national identity and express the national feeling; this goes back of course to the Vietnam defeat, perhaps the greatest of the setbacks. The Carter administration provided a response to this mood of a somewhat different kind before President Reagan came to power. The psychological need in America, which I think President Carter fulfilled, was the need Americans felt to feel virtuous. So many people told them how wicked they were; they had been oppressing the Third World, they had been bullying small peoples in Southeast Asia, resorting excessively to the use of force, and it was widely said—not only outside America, but by a large section of opinion in America itself—that America was not playing a virtuous role in the world but was supporting the wrong causes. People wanted to be told again this was not so, that America still had a moral mission in the world, that Americans were good people. This is one of the feelings that President Carter sought in his human rights campaign; people were glad to hear that America was, after all, a great champion of human rights, that America's adversaries in the Communist world and the Third World, who presumed to criticize America, had deplorable records in the fields, that Americans had no reason to be ashamed of themselves but every reason for self-respect.

President Reagan, I think, is satisfying another national urge of a slightly different kind, which is the urge to feel strong. This is a response to the growth of Russian power, to the various demonstrations of American impotence (the Vietnam War, the 1973-1974 oil crisis, the Iranian hostage crisis) around the world in the 1970s. People want to feel again that America is a militarily powerful country, that it can flex its muscles, that it cannot be pushed around. So when President Reagan came to power, particularly in the early period, there followed a great deal of rhetoric which satisfied this need.

It may be that it was psychologically necessary and even right in terms of American domestic politics that these needs should be satisfied. To hold the country together, to restore national morale and confidence, these feelings had to be expressed. But the policies that have satisfied these national feelings at home have exacerbated America's problems abroad. The European allies, when they heard the rhetoric of the Reagan administration—the muscle flexing, the dramatic increase of defense expenditures, the revival of talk about military intervention, the Star Wars speech, the unfriendly attitude, initially to arms control negotiations—were alarmed.

The rejection of detente in America, which began in the Carter period, not with the advent of President Reagan, has been basically unpopular in Europe. Detente even today is a good word, and has never ceased to be a good word in Europe. Detente for Western Europeans means the understandings that they have reached with the Soviet Union over frontiers, over trade, and over arms control that have produced a more relaxed and peaceful atmosphere in Europe than what existed before; most Western European opinion regards the preservation of detente as a good thing, believes that American policies of rejection of detente were wrong and have contributed to a deterioration of the international climate. It is not my business to pursue this issue for its own sake, except to say that one of the exacerbating factors in the alliance has been that both President Reagan and President Carter—perhaps inevitably, perhaps rightly—in their foreign policies have been responding primarily to a domestic need, and in doing so have in some ways exacerbated the problem of America's relations with its allies.

A fourth point: the President of the United States is so important that America is vulnerable to the particular character of the person who occupies the office. Who the President of the United States is, what sort of person he is, whether he is going to go down well with foreigners or not, is very important. Sometimes the incumbent proves to be an asset to America internationally, sometimes he does not. If one looks back over history, many American Presidents have been regarded as a beacon light in the rest of the world: Lincoln, for example; Woodrow Wilson, for all his faults; Franklin Roosevelt; John F. Kennedy. These American leaders commanded great prestige and authority in Europe, people looked to them and to the moral leadership they could give.

But many of the American figures have occupied the presidency and haven't been up to that. Lord Bryce in his book on *The American Commonwealth* has a chapter which is entitled "Why Great Men Do Not Get Elected President of the United States." That is a little unfair; there have been some great men elected or men whose greatness becomes apparent after they are elected. But sometimes the persons who occupy the office are very ordinary, and sometimes alien from the point of view of foreigners. President Reagan, though he is obviously in many respects a very successful President domestically, has a style that has alienated many Europeans; and this was also true, though much less so, of President Carter—a very locally based American figure, a more provincial and less cosmopolitan figure, less congenial to European expectations than previous postwar American Presidents had been.

Now there is a fifth point that will be the last one: this is the concern that has always been expressed in Europe, but is being expressed more now than it had ever been before, about the President's powers of patronage, or what is called "the spoils system," the way in which the President is able to appoint a vast number of political figures not only to high but also to medium rank offices. As you know in the United Kingdom this is not the way the system operates. The ministers of the cabinet, the foreign secretary, the chancellor of the exchequer, and so on, are members of Parliament and though the prime minister appoints them, she can only appoint them from a limited range of major figures in the party who are members of Parliament. The civil service is a wholly professional bureaucracy; the top figures in the civil service are people who have spent all their lives in this role as professional bureaucrats, and this is the pattern in all Western European countries.

In the United States, of course as everybody knows, a great many of these very important appointments are political appointments, and what this frequently results in—not always but what it often results in—is what from the European perspective appears to be government by amateurs, government by people who have just come in to the job, who take a long time to learn the job, and often are inexperienced. It is not, of course, always so. Sometimes political appointees are persons of great experience relevant to their jobs. Moreover, there have been times when Europeans have admired the so-called "spoils system" and sought to learn from it. For example, the Kennedy administration made a great impact on European thinking by its ability to bring talent into Washington, to appoint to high office people who had a great deal of knowledge and skill. This created a lot of envy in Europe and there were even attempts to imitate it. When Harold Wilson won the 1964 election for the Labour Party he tried in Britain, in a rather ineffective way, to imitate the American system in a minor way and there has always been talk about trying to get a sort of White House staff at number 10 Downing Street and to strengthen the prime minister's position to make political appointments. It is not uncommon for ministers to appoint political advisors to their staffs in the British system, but these are junior positions.

In the last few years especially, there has been a great deal of complaint in Europe about this situation, a feeling that many of the people around American Presidents recently have not got the experience and judgment necessary. A great deal of the effort of American foreign policy, it seems, has been devoted to getting out of the pits into which the United States has fallen through inexperience and lack of judgment. This is the sort of thing one hears discussed frequently in Europe today. It is not so much because the system has changed or because the people being appointed today are very different from what they were earlier; it is rather just that other countries today are more vulnerable than in earlier periods to what the United States does, and feel the effects of it more when something goes wrong.

I would welcome your questions and comments.

Question: Two points very briefly. Is there any perception that this thirst for moral approval domestically is much older than Vietnam? After all, saving the world for democracy in World War I and isolationism even before World War I were based in some measure at least on the fact that we were morally so much superior to those evil people in Europe. It's an old, old aspect which Reagan keeps playing in moral superiority of Americans and Westerners generally to the Soviet Union. He plays the chord very frequently. Is there any perception that this is more than simply the Vietnam thing? The second question is whether there is any concern in Europe for the strong ongoing relationship between the President and the press and media as a whole than is often so in the British scene?

Professor Bull: I agree with you that the belief of Americans that they are especially virtuous and that they have a moral mission in the world and that they are better than other people, at least in their political intentions, or certainly than some other people is not something that just turned up the other day. It is a belief that has been there a long time, indeed from the very beginning. What I think is newer is the feeling of the need to demonstrate this. I think it was taken for granted in earlier years. When Woodrow Wilson wanted to save the world for democracy, he was not doing that in response to some doubt that may have existed about American virtue. But the Vietnam War, the criticism of America by Third World leaders, the credence given in the West itself to the idea that America is the great oppressor, the arch neo-colonial power—something not only being said by foreigners but by Americans also—this has offended a longstanding idea of America as a virtuous country. It was this that it was necessary to correct, a function that Carter performed.

I think there is a deeper point here. Kissinger said recently somewhere that in the nineteenth century Americans used to think that Europeans were steeped in power politics and somewhat wicked because they were always having wars and engaging in Machiavellian plots against one another, whereas America was going to correct this with Woodrow Wilsonian virtue. On the other hand, Europeans thought Americans were moralistic and naive and failed to attend to the realities of power. Now, however, America and Europe have reversed their roles. Now it is America that is deeply involved in power politics, and has to compromise moral purpose with power, whereas the Europeans are sitting on the sidelines in the way that the Americans used to in the nineteenth century, and are accusing the Americans of being steeped in power politics, while the Americans are accusing the Europeans of having their heads in the clouds. That is an exaggeration; Europe is NOT quite like what America was in the nineteenth century, but there is something in it. The reason why America now needs to be reassured about its virtue is that it is heavily involved, steeped in power politics in a way that it was not in the nineteenth century. Because America is all the time having to concern itself with a struggle with the Soviet Union, with matching Soviet military power, with intervening all around the world to contain the Soviet's expansion, while Europeans are not, America has become vulnerable to the charge of not being virtuous, and wants to be told that its virtue is still intact.

Question: Stanley Hoffmann has made an effort in this country to make sure that we understand the foreignness of foreigners. I don't think he understands Americans. Who in Britain today, if anyone, is a successor to Lord Bryce? To me, that is the finest book written by a Britisher who did understand this country. And what is the status of American studies? Is America understood at Oxford, and at lesser institutions in Britain, and particularly in the press? I close with two examples which constantly disturb me—the fact that the British don't understand the vast difference in our political spectrum from theirs; the fact that it is not accidental we have no labor party very deeply rooted in our culture. And also the sort of argument E.H. Carr was always making that America is some twenty years behind Britain and give her time, she'll catch up. No, no. The patterns of history are totally different. Is that being deeply explored at the academic level anywhere in Great Britain?

Professor Bull: Well, I don't think there is a successor to Bryce or to his book *The American Commonwealth* and I don't think any contemporary British interpreter of the United States is as important as Bryce was. One could refer to one person who was a later exponent of American studies in Britain, now dead, Dennis Brogan, who wrote a book called *The American Political System* which was the sort of book that people read in my student days if they wanted to find out about America. I think that was an important book. Louis Heren, the *Times* correspondent, produced a book called *The New American Commonwealth,* which was meant to be an update of Bryce's book. It's a nice little book but it doesn't have the profound qualities that Bryce's book did have. American studies are much more widely pursued in British universities than they once were. In Oxford there are two chairs of American history, one for a visiting American historian, which was occupied recently by Professor Norman Graebner of the University of Virginia, the Harmsworth Professorship, and another for a permanent incumbent, the Rhodes Professorship of American History. I would say there are probably a dozen or so British universities that have chairs of American history or institutions, possibly more. But there is not enough study of America and I think people are inclined to think, wrongly, that they know enough about America. America is so prominent to us all the time, there is such a constant American presence in Britain, that people imagine that they have an instinctive knowledge of America, and don't need to study it in the way they need to study other countries. I heard recently Peter Jay, who was of course British ambassador in Washington, complain about the fact that within the British foreign service there was no special training of a corps of American specialists. When you enter the foreign service, you are asked whether you want to be an Arab specialist, a Russian specialist, a Chinese specialist and so on. But there is no American category. People think that America is something that everybody knows about. Jay was arguing that this was a serious problem in Britain's relations with the United States.

Question: Can I interrupt to say here that we have had since World War II prime ministers whose mothers were Americans and both Churchill and Macmillan took the line that there was no need. I mean when these questions were raised, Churchill and Macmillan said this is ridiculous. We know all about it. And perhaps he did, his mother being a Hoosier from Indiana. Not all of us have the luck of having American mothers, therefore it isn't so easy.

Question: Some of us have American wives, an enormous help.

Question: One observation about American studies. At Oxford in my time in the school of history there was one subject in American history which was slavery and secession and now I know that that is expanding. One thing that did strike me though this summer in England, and I suspect if I'd have looked in the American press I'd have read about it too, and that is that neither country seems to cover each other very well. I mean the coverage in the British press that I was seeing in June was primarily about what we call the rating game; you wouldn't have known there was much else going on in this country.

I would like to ask you one other question which is this. You mentioned a spoils system and the professionalism of British diplomacy. Has that changed? The reason I ask that question is because the British ambassador was here two weeks ago, and at an Oxford dinner, informal and humorous and what not, we started off with a few anecdotes and he progressed into unabashed Thatcherism which seemed to me to be sort of out of place for a diplomat. Is that new? I mean, now do British diplomats endorse the policy of the prime minister? It was a political speech, that's what it was.

Professor Bull: If the question is, do British diplomats abroad feel that they must endorse the policy of the British government, I would think the answer to that question is yes, that is their job, whether they like it or not. If the question is, do members of the British foreign service in fact stand united behind Mrs. Thatcher's ideas, I would think the answer is no. I myself think that Mrs. Thatcher is politically somewhat to the right of the views of what you might call the establishment, of most people in the Foreign Office, and perhaps the leading writers of the leading newspapers or people who go to meetings at Chatham House—those sorts of people. I think they would be at least privately critical of the heavily ideological anticommunist stance that Mrs. Thatcher takes and would want to see some moderation of that.

Question: Has the British support of the United States in certain particular cases weakened British political support in Europe?

Professor Bull: I don't think so because on most of the issues that have really mattered to the European Community countries at large, Britain actually has gone along with them. On the pipeline deal, for example, Mrs. Thatcher was supportive of the German Chancellor and of the French and stood with the Europeans rather than with the United States. On the general question of relations with the East and detente and arms control, the British government is more aligned with the European governments than with the United States, although you sometimes wouldn't be able to tell this from listening to Mrs. Thatcher's speeches. But the main emphasis has been upon the need for arms control conversations, the need to see the cruise missile question in the context of negotiations with the Soviet Union and so on. It's true that Mrs. Thatcher, in her speech in this country the other day, delivered a strong denunciation of the Soviet Union and wanted to be tougher than the other European countries over the Korean airline problem. But I don't think this policy has got Britain into trouble in Europe. We do not encounter today the sort of difficulty that used to arise twenty years ago, in the days of the arguments between Kennedy and de Gaulle, when it used to be said that Britain was an American Trojan horse and the reason why Britain ought to be kept out of the European Community was if it got in there it would just be doing the Americans' work for them. I don't think you do hear that among Europeans now because Britain is in the European Community. Although Britain is in some respects an unpopular member of the Community, it is unpopular not for that reason, but because of disagreements over agricultural policy, the Community budget and so on. I haven't myself heard recently the accusation that Britain is the European agent of the United States.

Question: You mentioned the spoils system in America as being different from the British system. In America in the last two elections the average person would hear the word "bureaucrat" and it would have a very pejorative meaning. And both the last Presidents ran against the American as controlled centrally from Washington by those wicked bureaucrats with the idea that that's not a good system. Now in Britain is your democracy any less participatory because you do have a professional civil service who, speaking simply, do run Britain?

Professor Bull: Yes, there is something in this line of criticism. There are many people in Britain who feel that Britain is too much in the hands of the professional civil servants, and that is why the British people, when they look at the American system, don't see it as being all bad. They have sometimes wanted to borrow from it. There have been articles in *The Times* recently, in just the last few days, criticizing the bureaucracy basically on the grounds that it wasn't possible to introduce talent from outside. It has even been argued that it ought to be possible in Britain to appoint as ministers of the crown persons from outside Parliament, to bring in someone and make him a minister and the cabinet ought not be restricted to members of Parliament. But of course you have got the possibility of doing that from members of the House of Lords. I think it is a defect, for example, with the professional foreign service, that people who spend their whole lives within this framework tend to get narrow perspectives and there is an argument for opening the door and letting people go in and out. Britain should learn from the United States in that respect. The trouble is that the American system often results in the appointment of people from outside who really have been put there to pay off political favors and not because they really are the people best for the job.

Question: In Britain or Australia has there been any discussion of the paralysis that hits the United States in both the executive and legislature for at least a year before the national elections? If so, are there any suggestions for solving it that have been discussed?

Professor Bull: Yes, in fact there is something going on in Australia that is related to this. The Labor government, which has just been elected in Australia, has a proposal to amend the Constitution so that elections would only be held every four years instead of every three years. There is a feeling that there is too much energy going into elections in Australia and that people once elected ought to stay for longer. That's connected with the point you're making. You are saying, or at least certainly a lot of people think, that too much energy of Americans goes into this whole business of elections. The 1984 election is already in progress in effect. This tends to dominate everything and the closer you get to the election the more issues have to be postponed because it won't be until after the election that anything can be decided. I can see that you might argue that this was a good thing because it meant that the more people are preoccupied with getting reelected the more they are going to have to operate within the democratic constraints. But it does militate often against efficiency and against getting things done. I don't imagine it can be changed though. Does anybody think it can be changed?

Narrator: If you add to that problem the year after a new administration comes in, well that doesn't leave you much time.

Question: Paralysis exists in both domestic policy and foreign policy, and both in the executive and the legislature.

Question: Yes, and the legislature is elected every two years.

Professor Bull: Of course in many countries there is legislation which requires the election campaign to be a short one; the virtue of the British election is that it's all over in a short time. Perhaps you can have legislation that would in some way restrict this. I don't think, however, that any legislation is going to stop people thinking about who will be the next President or trying to influence the choice, but maybe some aspects of this can be changed.

Question: The prime minister of Britain doesn't have an adversary relationship with Parliament because he is the head of the majority party and for that reason is prime minister. You mentioned party discipline. Could you comment on voting patterns in Britain, how much does the discipline of the parties reflect the wishes of all the people of the United Kingdom in your elections? Do seventy-five percent of the eligible voters vote? How does that compare vis-a-vis the American patterns of voting?

Professor Bull: Actually I just don't have the figures in my mind. I really don't know whether the percentage is higher in Britain or not. Of course in Australia they have compulsory voting. You've got to vote in Australia and so this is something that can't be measured. That's a defect inasmuch that whether a person votes or not is itself an index of how seriously he or she feels about the issue.

Narrator: I think it's right that the person most responsible for Professor Bull being here and contributing so much to the life of the Miller Center should ask the last question, Adam Watson.

Adam Watson: Well, I have this question, Hedley, which we've talked about before and on which I think people are interested to your views. A very common complaint of European political leaders and also

Australian and Japanese is that American decisions about foreign policy, let us say about the size for contributions to the IMF or how long you keep troops in the Lebanon or anything else, have to be hammered out through a whole restraining set of chains and checks and balances which were put into the Constitution in order to limit the power of the executive to a certain extent. Of course it was in reaction to the behavior of George III and so on and nobody is against these checks and balances, but one of the great difficulties which follows for the allies is that by the time the policy has been hammered out and traded off and arranged as part of a package compromised with some other piece of domestic legislation and squaring senator this and congressman that and taking it all through the interest groups and the lobbyists and everything else, once this huge domestic process has gone on and on policies are weakened. If someone like Bob Hawke of Australia comes along and says I don't like that, then should we go through the whole thing again because you, Bob Hawke, don't like page three—this is ridiculous. The impression of the allies is that Americans go through this process and they present this process after enormous difficulty to their allies and there is virtually no way either before or after, they are told, of changing it. The result is that the Americans are not the captains of a team leading the collective view of the alliance, they arrive unilaterally by this process at their decisions and then they tow the allies in what seems to proud old countries like Britain and France and proud new countries like Australia as somewhat arbitrary and in somewhat an ignominious manner. Now this is a well known comment of governments, isn't it? Would you like to talk about that?

Professor Bull: Yes, there is something very unwieldy about the American process. It can't be put into reverse; I've often thought that about arms control agreements going through the Senate. I think that the allies just have to live with this, but there are some compensations. There is one great virtue of the American system in dealing with allies and others and that is that it is completely open. There is no government in the world whose process of decisionmaking are as public and are as open to scrutiny and discussion as that of the United States. Britain and France are in a way closer even to the Soviet Union than they are to the United States in this respect. There is a public debate, and things are settled democratically in Britain, but the conception in American government of publishing information, of having everything open is much weaker in the other Western democracies than it is in the United States. And I think ultimately, this is an advantage to the allies in dealing with

America. The American system may be very complicated, it may be very difficult to tell what is going to happen at the end of the process, but at least it can be studied, the information is all there, and if the embassies in Washington want to take the trouble and follow all these things and find them out, they can. It's an open process and a country whose policies are determined secretively is in a much weaker position to create confidence in allies. The allies may not know where they stand, but at least the factors that will determine where they stand can be identified and studied.

Narrator: I'm sure I speak for all you in thanking Hedley Bull for this very stimulating and thoughtful presentation. If he's not an authority on the subject, somehow, as he began to think about it, he acquired that ability.

CHAPTER 2

THE PRESIDENT: A VIEW FROM OXFORD

Herbert G. Nicholas

Viewed either in its dignified or in its efficient capacity, the Presidency is the supreme unifying element in the American system of government. The Supreme Court may symbolize and dispense the justice under law without which the Union could not long survive. Congress may provide voice and sinew for the multiple elements that make up the national mixture. But it is the President who speaks and acts for the nation as a whole, who takes at his inauguration the prescribed oath to 'preserve, protect and defend the Constitution of the United States', and to whom the nation looks, when all else fails, to take the decisions needed to preserve the Union against internal disintegration or external threat. Fathers do not bring up their children to be members of Congress, nor do many nourish the hope of seeing their offspring on the Supreme Court, but there have been few log cabins that, in popular imagination at least, did not command an avenue which terminated in the White House.

To have been born of American parents, to have been fourteen years a resident of the U.S.A., and thirty five years of age—these modest constitutional qualifications leave the career open to almost all talents, and even the extra-constitutional requirements do not close it to many. Since 1960 it has not been necessary to be a Protestant, though it would be a rash candidate who professed no Christian faith at all. It is still essential to be either a Democrat or a Republican. (Of those candidates in recent times who were not, LaFollette in 1924 came closest to success, and that was not very close.) It is, apparently, helpful to be or have been a lawyer; two-thirds of Presidents have been, while over half have had military experience. Two-thirds have served in one house or other of Congress, and a surprising number (thirteen) have been Vice Presidents. But considering the nature of the chief executive's office it is surprising that fewer than a third have had previous experience of federal office-holding and only fifteen have been state governors.

However, the qualifications, formal and informal, for the Presidency do not give much clue to the essential nature of the job. This is *the* great American institution, its creation arguably the greatest achievement of the American political genius (what other country has been able to operate an elective monarchy for over 200 years without interruption?), the quadrennial contest for it *the* drama of American politics, the enjoyment of it perhaps the most exacting, as it is certainly the most lonely, task that any democratically elected official in the world can undertake. The spotlight of publicity never leaves the incumbent, or his family; successive Presidents, by seeking to cash in on an insatiable public curiosity about every detail of their private lives, from their golf handicap to their digestive processes, have left an ever smaller area of activity the incumbent can call his own. The White House combines the glamour of a palace, albeit a small one, with the intimacy of a home, and it is precisely that blend of the official and the personal which gives the Presidency its peculiar potency. As Bagehot said of Queen Victoria's monarchy, "it brings down the pride of sovereignty to the level of petty life' and 'sweetens politics by the seasonable addition of nice and pretty events.' Possibly the domestic round at the White House is not quite as pretty (or at any rate as glamorous) as at Windsor, but in an age more sophisticated than Victoria's the American President may gain even more from the combination of being both a family man and a (four-year) prince. He is after all both monarch and prime minister, both head of state and head of government—a partisan government (he has won election on a party label) and yet a government of all the people.

This imposes strains. The dignified aspects of the office may call for attributes which the politican may lack. Not all of Lyndon Johnson's personal foibles were as well suited to the state rooms of the White House as to the *couloirs* of the Senate. A reforming President may arouse resentments, warranted or not, which may stand in his way when he has to speak to or for the whole nation; Woodrow Wilson and Franklin Roosevelt were victims of that. Every Presidency offers examples of failures to bring into identical focus the two images of the office. On the whole, however, what is remarkable about the American experience is the success that the United States has achieved in establishing and maintaining the democratic ideal of an elected monarch. Not every President succeeds in effecting the perfect combination of popular appeal and supra-party stature of a Lincoln, though Harry Truman in our time has demonstrated how this is still within the reach of a man of superficially ordinary talent. But time and time again at moments of crisis Presidents have been able to draw upon the inherited resources of their office to evoke from the country a response which transcends anything that mere party or personality could elicit. If the dual character of the office carries certain hazards it also confers certain unique advantages.

There is no royal road to the Presidency. The office is filled every four years by the man who is successful first in winning his party's nomination and then in carrying the ensuing election. In one sense this is a truly winnowing process. The contest is long and intense—never less than from winter to autumn—and involves contests in presidential primaries spread over five months or more, reaches its first peak in the nominating convention in July and August, and then culminates in an all-out offensive from September to November. An athlete's stamina, a chameleon's adaptability, a lavish war chest, a loyal but not overly exclusive campaign team, a capacity both to elicit and to transcend party loyalty—these are the desirable attributes of a successful candidate. They are not, unfortunately, enough to guarantee success in office, as Presidents from Harding to Carter have discovered. For life in the White House there are other, increasingly essential, qualifications, in particular experience of executive office, which can actually be a handicap in the campaign (because executives have to disappoint as well as please), knowledge of the Washington establishment (once upon a time each President made his own, like Andrew Jackson; now he has to cope with a permanent nexus of office and influence), and finally and perhaps most indispensably, knowledge of and feeling for the international world beyond America's borders.

Obviously the paragon has not yet been made who is at all points equal to the challenges of the Presidency (and who can also get himself elected). In his absence there has been a strong temptation to fall back on the arts of opinion-manipulation for which their practitioners (and their critics) claim so much. Candidates can be packaged, Presidents can be sold, underdogs can become top dogs if the right strategies are adopted—this is the 'nothing is impossible' world of political advertising and public relations. It is permissible to doubt how much these artful practitioners can in fact deliver (cf. Ronald Reagan's low poll even in his so-called landslide victory of 1984), though of course it has to be admitted that where the margin of victory is small enough (0.2 per cent in 1960 for Kennedy) any factor can be adjudged crucial. The measuring rod which can assess such aids to victory has yet to be invented. But it is permissible to ask why so much dependence, at such expense, has come to be placed upon such meretricious and dubious mechanisms.

Part of the answer lies undoubtedly in the mesmeric effect of television, especially commercial television, since 1948. The seeming success of the new medium in selling sentiment, thrills, and detergents to the viewer encouraged the conviction that it could be similarly employed to sell him a President. Despite the gigantic deployment of talent and funds in the service of this operation it is by no means certain that the medium has produced the results attributed to it.[1] It is hard to think of candidates less 'telegenic' than Lyndon Johnson or Nixon or more photographically appealing than John Lindsay, yet the screen did not thwart the designs of the first two or rescue the fortunes of the third. What it has done, indubitably, is to heighten the hazards, the burdens, the superficiality and the costs of campaigning; the hazards because a gaffe on TV is a gaffe registered by millions; the burdens because TV has been superimposed on the existing chores of campaigning; the superficiality because the image, pre-packaged, can easily override the argument, however cogent; the costs because television time is prodigiously expensive.

But behind the obvious appeal of TV as the all-purpose, wonder-working gimmick lies a more fundamental change in the nature of presidential candidacies. As recently as Franklin D. Roosevelt a candidate won his nomination and conducted his campaign primarily through the mechanism as well as in the name of his party. Since 1952 he has been, by comparison, a lonely runner. Eisenhower did not win the nomination or the election as a Republican Party leader. He could have had the nomination of either party; he won on a broad wave of support that derived from his personal and wartime popularity. Eight years later John F. Kennedy returned the White House to the Democrats, but not by working through the 'regular' party organization. Instead he assembled his own team and financed it very largely by his own fortune. In the campaign, as in the White House, he kept his 'New Frontiersmen' distinct from the old party hacks. Lyndon Johnson, apprenticed as a New Dealer and deeply dyed in the party politics of House and Senate, nevertheless, when he campaigned for himself in 1964, built his own organization, on his Kennedy inheritance, rather than on the party in the country. Nixon, more than any of his predecessors, ran his own campaign with his own loyalists, from their own headquarters in New York City, in 1968 and 1972. At the opposite extreme George McGovern, Nixon's 1972 opponent, created his 'children's crusade' of ruthless idealists who were as much at odds with the conventional Democratic Party as with the Republicans. Carter's image in 1976 was in many ways a more conservative one, but he no less created his own team, basically Georgian, to win the nomination and, in office, to run the government; there were few debts outstanding when victory was won, either by White House to Congress or vice versa.

Reagan in 1980 built his campaign around a team of carefully selected advisers, some from his base in California politics, some of them veterans of the Nixon presidential years. With these he conducted a highly personal offensive in virtually every presidential primary and by his sequence of successes arrived at the convention with the nomination assured.

As these examples suggest, in such a situation it does no harm to the presidential candidate for him to have generous campaign resources of his own. If he will not need them after nomination (and they may well be a help even then), he will certainly need them in the primaries. The public will not hold it against him, and his entourage will sleep better and work harder if they know that, come success or failure, his cheques will not bounce. That does not mean that the Presidency can be bought. As the fate of Nelson Rockefeller, who never quite made it to the altar, reminds us, it takes more than a dowry to make a bride. But what money can do for a candidate is to emancipate him from hand-to-mouth improvisations and dependencies, enable him to plan strategically rather than tactically, help him to negotiate with 'the interests' for a position of governmental independence.

Meanwhile, and irrespective of the personal independence of individual candidates, the weak, and incoherent American party has resulted in the development of a more detached, indeed isolated, Presidency, whose burdens have grown greater while its base has grown smaller. In such a situation, the President's Cabinet is of little help; British observers should not be deceived by the similarity of name into thinking that this is any kind of equivalent to Bagehot's 'hyphen which joins,' and 'a buckle which fastens.' Far better to think of it as Professor Richard Fenno,* its most authoritative modern analyst, describes it, as 'the lengthened shadow of the Presidency.' It is indeed 'the President's Cabinet.' As such it is, very properly, not known to the Constitution. Nor are the extra-constitutional guidelines very clear or rigid. Its official

*Richard F. Fenno, *The President's Cabinet*, p. 5 (Cambridge, Mass., Harvard University Press, 1959.)

membership is that of the heads of the established executive departments, those that have Secretaries, from State to Agriculture. But if membership is defined in terms of actual attendance, Cabinet membership is a much more fluid matter. Other agency heads will be called in as often and for as long as required. The Attorney General and the Director of the Office of Management and Budget (OMB) are likely to be regulars and it is a rare meeting that will not be attended by one or more members of the President's own White House staff. The result is a rather unreal collectivity, a body which can very rarely develop independent powers of deliberation, still less a will or policy of its own. And this for a very good reason: its members are there, ultimately, because the President has selected them to carry out his policies, not because they represent elements in his party or even sections of his constituents. Indeed, although at the inception of a new administration a President may take care, in making his principal appointments, that considerations of representativeness have due weight—that Catholics, Jews, Negroes, Southwesterners, women, trade unionists, right-wingers, left-wingers, etc. all have their place, two other considerations will inescapably dominate his subsequent replacements—loyalty and competence. Only the strongest of Presidents like Lincoln can tolerate rivals within their administration; only the most indulgent, like Franklin Roosevelt, can put up with executives who fall down on the job. Thus most Cabinets will consist not of broad-based, interchangeable, debate-minded all-rounders (the theory at least underlying British Cabinet membership) but of two recognizable types: those members who are experts in their own field—foreign affairs, say, or budget management—and those who represent a certain constituency—labour, agriculture, etc.—which the President cannot afford to ignore. The first group are unlikely to venture far outside their own specialities, the second are generally indifferent to considerations which do not have an immediate impact upon their constituents.

All this reduces the value of the Cabinet either as a sounding board which the President can use or as a forum in which a critic can bring to the President's notice any of those topics that monarchs, elected or unelected, prefer not to hear about. Memoirs of Cabinet members are replete with evidence of the barrenness of their collective deliberations and the assiduity with which each tries to catch the President's private ear after the plenary session is over. *Per contra* the open voicing of disagreements between Cabinet members which by British standards is a relatively frequent feature of American government, will have proportionately less serious consequences. Of course it is always better if members of an administration present a solid front to the world, but where it is recognized that Cabinet members have little responsibility for extra-departmental policy and do have an inescapable obligation to serve their constituents, in Congress or the country, the damage, if not the brouhaha, that ensues from these open breaches of unanimity can generally be sustained.

The unserviceability of the Cabinet as an instrument either of deliberation or co-ordination has led to an increased reliance on other devices. It was in the area of foreign and defence policy that the Cabinet's inadequacies—its diffuseness, its loose-lipped indifference to consistency or security—first necessitated the creation of another organ to advise the President and co-ordinaate what the main departments were doing. This was the National Security Council, set up in 1947 in the wake of the U.S.A.'s wartime experience and also in emulation of what Americans had observed, as members of the wartime alliance, of the Defence Committee of the British Cabinet. The N.S.C. consists essentially of the President, the Vice-President (a recognition in push-button warfare days of the need to try and guarantee continuity of command in the event of presidential incapacity), and the Secretaries of State and Defense; not the least of its strengths derives from its being serviced by a small and highly competent permanent staff directed by the Presidents assistant for National Security Affairs. The N.S.C. has introduced order, reflection, and planning into areas where decisions were previously taken too readily by hunch or departmental muscle. Even so, it would be a great mistake to regard it as an institution with any strength in its own right. When Nixon decided in December 1972 to try and end the Vietnam war by unleashing the whirlwind bombardment of North Vietnam he did not consult the N.S.C.; indeed the N.S.C. had not met in more than six months. It is essentially a presidential convenience, a device to be used, or ignored, as presidential taste or prudence may dictate.

Even more is this true of such experiments as have been made with a counterpart, the so-called Domestic Council, such as Nixon created in 1970, or the five Cabinet Councils set up by Reagan in 1981. They too had staff and the equivalent of a secretary. But they were conduits for decision-making as often by-passed as used, irregular in function, uncertain as to power. The truth is that every President likes to think he is running a freshly-minted model of orderly administration and each one blots the beauty of his organisational charts under the stresses of actual decision-making.

The President, all the same, is only one man. He must have assistance. In 1861 Abraham Lincoln had embarked on a Presidency and a civil war with only two secretaries and a young ex-newspaperman to sort the mail. By 1933 Franklin Roosevelt had become aware that he would need something more than this if the United States government was going to cope with the Depression, and in 1939 he stabilized his expanded establishment in the form of the Executive Office of the President, in effect a White House secretariat that would enable him to exercise some measure of effective control over the sprawling ganglion which constitutes the federal government. Although repeatedly modified (generally in the direction of expansion) since Roosevelt's time, the structure still stands on his foundations. At its centre is the White House Office which serves the President directly and personally through his principal assistants or advisers, who will always include a press secretary, a presidential counsel, an appointments secretary, a congressional liaison officer, a speech writer, and an adviser on national security who will also be secretary to the N.S.C. Most Presidents have needed in addition an *alter ego,* lynchpin to this wheel, who could be their completely trusted confidant and right arm—Woodrow Wilson's Colonel House, Roosevelt's Harry Hopkins, Eisenhower's Sherman Adams, Kennedy's Theodore Sorenson, Nixon's Bob Haldeman, Carter's Hamilton Jordan, Reagan's James Baker—but each has had his own method of organizing the office as a whole, from Roosevelt's 'creative chaos' to Eisenhower's army-style channels of command. Presidents have similarly differed as to the range of functions which they have wished to keep under their personal control, though most modern administrations have agreed that foreign policy is an area which the White House can never leave to the formally responsible department, State. In consequence the President's foreign policy assistant, be he a Bundy, a Kissinger, or a Brzezinski, is always more than a liaison officer, or even a watchdog to see that the President's policies are properly executed. He is, at the very least, something very close to being a second Secretary of State; sometimes like Kissinger he is the *de facto* Secretary whatever his location.

The expansion, in size and complexity, of the Executive Office of the President has led to a good deal of loose talk about the Presidency having become 'institutionalized'. This idea enjoyed particular currency during Eisenhower's presidential incapacities when the impression was deftly conveyed by James Hagerty, his press officer, that the work of the office could be conducted in the chief's absence through the machinery of Cabinet and aides. In reality this fiction was sustained only by some dubiously constitutional exercise of power on the part of Sherman Adams, and the President's remarkable powers of recuperation. The truth is that the Presidency is far too personal an office ever to be truly institutionalized,[2] and indeed, by Whitehall standards, the White House Office is even less institutionalized than No. 10. There is almost total fluidity in the top appointments, which change with each President, and hardly less flexibility in the shape and organization of the whole—in each case for the same reason, a new President's need to run things his own way.

The most nearly institutionalized part of the Presidency is something which in Whitehall would be housed in the Treasury. From 1921 to 1929 a Bureau of the Budget was indeed housed in the U.S. Treasury, but as part of the White House reforms of that year it was brought directly under presidential control, with the responsibility not merely of preparing annual budgets but also of using the power of the purse to keep the executive departments under tighter control. Reorganized and renamed in 1970 as the Office of Management and Budget (O.M.B.), the office is the drafting agency for the President's executive orders and proclamations and, even more important, is the clearing-house through which each department's proposals for new legislation must pass before they can be presented to Congress for its consideration. If there is a single, all-purpose institution of administrative control in Washington, this is it.

The figure at the apex of this pyramid, the human official in whose service and likeness this apparatus is constructed, is pre-eminently a man of power. This is something that follows from the size and might of the United States and from his position as the country's chief executive. But because his is a *constitutional* power we still have to ask exactly what it amounts to. Discrepant answers echo back to us from previous holders of the office. 'The President is at liberty, both in law and conscience', wrote Woodrow Wilson, 'to be as big a man as he can. His capacity will set the limit.' 'I sit here all day,'' said Harry Truman, 'trying to persusade people to do the things they ought to have sense enough to do without my persuading them. That's all the powers of the President amount to.' The Presidency, of course, has not stood still, either from Wilson's time to Truman's, or since. But its movement, until the excesses of Watergate were exposed, was almost wholly in one direction—towards self-aggrandizement. If Wilson sounded expansionary and Truman frustrated, it is because the one wrote when the pressures of the office and the aspirations of its holder were still comparatively modest, and the second registered his ironic protest when squeezed between constitutionalist critics and impatient clients. They reflect the contrast between an America with a modestly reforming government on a virtually island continent and an America whose daily bread and hourly security are inescapably dependent on decisions taken in the White House, often in response to happenings a hemisphere away.

In domestic politics this has led to an expectation of and a dependence on presidential leadership which seems irreversible. There is no evidence that in face of the vastly greater demands made on modern government Congress can itself provide a substitute for presidential leadership. The United States will never see in the White House another Ulysses S. Grant, with his conviction that the Presidency was 'a purely administrative office.' Indeed the Constitution itself forbids as much. Why else the provisions for presidential messages and presidential vetoes? Even Ford in his posture of presidential modesty after Watergate reached out for the veto on 66 occasions in two years and had fewer than 1 in 5 of them overruled. The constitutional battle is therefore joined on a comparatively narrow front.

A limited front, but within its limits, a confused and uncertain one. Thus the so-called legislative veto has been utilized by Congress since 1932, but has vastly increased, in frequency and significance, with the rise in Congressional assertiveness which the 'imperial presidencies' of Johnson and Nixon provoked. The legislative veto is a statutory provision that allows one or both houses of Congress to disapprove or hold in abeyance an action of the executive branch. At first sight it seems a clear shifting of the constitutional frontier in favour of Congress. The legislative veto has nevertheless survived presidential protests and has not yet been found unconstitutional by the Supreme Court. The reason is not far to seek. The restrictions that the veto imposes are the reverse side of the coin to the powers that Congress delegates. This was well illustrated by the history of impoundment. Nixon's refusal to spend money that Congress had voted for programmes of which he disapproved provoked the legislature into passing the 1974 Impoundment Control Act. But this did not prohibit impoundment as such; instead it recognised the power of the President to defer the spending of appropriated funds, but made such deferral subject to a Congressional resolution. In other words it recognised that the boundaries of presidential and congressional power had to be re-drawn. It did not seek a total acquisition of territory for either side, and in fact left it for future usage to decide whether the effect was to curb the President's independence or to concede some of the legislature's dearly cherished control of the purse.

The truth is that such intricate and ragged disputes are unlikely to yield to neat or merely legal solutions. What is ultimately at issue is the power of the President, working through public opinion, to get Congress to see things his way, with his formal constitutional and legal instruments mere ancillaries to his basic ability—or lack of it—to move the nation and its elected representatives by persuasion. Whether, beyond that, he has some kind of extra-constitutional residue of power to 'save' the nation, in the event of a congressional failure to act, is a somewhat scholastic question, much agitated at the time of the New Deal and always capable of being resuscitated in moments of crisis, but belonging ultimately to the realm of abstraction rather than practical politics. If crisis demands action and the right President is there to take it, he will act, and Congress and the courts will ratify his course afterwards (or disallow it after it has ceased to matter, like the disallowment of the N.R.A. in 1935). If the crisis does not warrant it or the wrong President is in charge, he will be impeached. The problem here is ultimately not a constitutional but a political one—whether a President can establish and maintain, either by personal authority or through his leadership of his party, a response from Congress which will sustain him not just at one moment or another but throughout the years which are needed to promulgate and carry through a policy.

In the area of foreign (and in this I include defence) policy the factors at work are different. In the first place the decline of party, so complicating and, as it were, debilitating, in domestic policy, does not have comparable consequences here. Party has seldom been a clear or clarifying factor in American foreign policy debates and its weakening has done little to diminish the President's potentialities in this sphere. Secondly, whereas the nineteenth-century President was more likely to meet a crisis on the domestic than on the foreign front, in the twentieth century the exact reverse is true. The domestic norm is still that of a predictable course of events at which both President and Congress can make reasonable guesses and for which both are equipped by previous experience. Where foreign affairs are concerned there is no norm; there is a permanent latent crisis. This is grimly symbolized by the 'black box' which accompanies a modern President wherever he goes and which contains the cryptograms he would employ if he had to press the nuclear button. There is no black box, there are no cryptograms, there is no nuclear button where domestic policies are concerned.

The power of the President in foreign affairs has received such striking demonstration in the era of the Cold War that it has seemed to some observers that there are, in effect, two Presidencies. Presidents who have been thwarted or defeated by Congress on their domestic programmes have succeeded time and time again in persuading Congress to acquiesce in their foreign policies. It was on its triumphs—or its excesses—in foreign policy that the 'Imperial Presidency' of the 1960s and '70s was built. This concept of the President as a solo virtuoso was almost certainly not shared by the Founding Fathers who envisaged the constitutional provision about seeking the 'advice and consent' of the Senate as committing the President to utilizing that chamber as a kind of council of state where foreign affairs were concerned. The Senators were after all to be the authorized spokesmen for the constituent parts of the Union. When there were only thirteen states and twenty six Sentors, and when foreign policy-making lacked day-to-day urgency, such a system might have worked—though, significantly perhaps, it was not seriously tried even at the outset. But as the federation grew and Senators multiplied, consultation shrank to the bare level required to meet the inescapable constitutional requirement that the President 'make Treaties, provided two-thirds of the Senators present concur' (Article II, Section ii, §2). Even so, as long as foreign policy revolved around the treaty-making process, the Senate Cerberus was a monster that every President had to respect and mollify. Even in the twentieth century, down to the time of Truman, the President had to measure his actions in foreign policy by the pace of the Senate—this despite the fact that by now foreign policy had acquired an urgency and priority unconceived of in 1789.

What emancipated the Presidency? It is hard to doubt that it was the invention of the atom bomb. Its potentialities for swift and total destruction, the problems of devising a safe and secret procedure of control, its early acquisition by a rival sovereign state—all this put into the President's hands a power which, whether he wanted it or not, he could not lodge elsewhere. It increased his stature and exclusiveness overnight. And although this was a weapon of war, its deadly 'brightness of a thousand suns' irradiated the President's peacetime diplomacy as well. Foreign policy-making henceforth was inevitably conducted in a new awareness of how swiftly irreversible a faulty step could be. The diplomacy of the Cuban missile crisis was not something which could be accommodated to traditional constitutional processes.

It is open to debate whether it was by historical coincidence or by the logic of its own implications, but, whichever it was, the atom bomb was evolved and, so to say, administered in the context of alliance diplomacy. The President who thus acquired an absolute weapon also involved his country in a set of permanent alliance commitments that had no parallel in American history. And just as only the President could control the bomb, so only the President could effectively run NATO and the U.S.A.'s other diplomatic-military arrangements whenever comparable elements of urgency and secrecy were involved.

The constitutional underpinnings of this new, exalted, and emancipated Presidency were already available once the lawyers and historians started to look for them. Perhaps the most adaptable and convenient formula was the one inherent in the deceptively simple label which the Constitution conferred on the President in making him 'Commander-in-Chief' of the Army, Navy, and militia (Article II, Section ii, §1). Out of this Lincoln had conjured the power to impose a blockade, raise a volunteer army, expand the regular army and navy, suspend *habeas corpus,* introduce conscription, and issue the Emancipation Proclamation—all without congressional authorization.

Second only to this was the undermining of the Senate's exclusive control over treaty-making. The instrument to hand for this purpose was the President's claimed right to negotiate 'executive agreements' with foreign powers. This had a long and respectable lineage, from the Rush-Bagot agreement of 1817 establishing disarmament in the Great Lakes to the Lansing-Ishii agreement of 1917 which recognized Japan's 'special rights' in China. But it was World War II and its aftermath that really brought the executive agreement into its own, as the points of contact and potential friction between the U.S.A. and other powers multiplied, and so necessitated a faster and more flexible range of negotiating instruments than the treaty-making process could provide. The numbers negotiated have now run into thousands, the ratio of executive agreements to treaties has risen from 1.5:1 to 15:1, and the courts have fully upheld their validity and enforceability in law. It is by such agreements that the U.S.A. maintains many of its bases overseas, provides much of its military assistance to its allies, and indeed operates a major part of its alliance diplomacy. This does not mean, of course, that anything that required a treaty can now be accomplished by executive agreement. There persists a consensus about what is 'expected' by Senate and foreign negotiators alike, a consensus determined partly by precedent, partly by prestige. The future of the Panama Canal, like its original conception, is still felt to need a senatorial blessing. But the range of topics for which a presidential laying on of hands suffices has grown longer every year.

In these twilight zones of modern diplomacy it was not to be expected that the other congressional prerogative (shared between House and

Senate), the right to declare war, could retain much vitality. Hardly was the ink dry on this clause of the Constitution (Article I, Section viii, §11) than the illusoriness of its claims became apparent. In order to occur war does not have to be 'declared.' It can come, as the universe came to Margaret Fuller, and simply insist on being accepted. In only one instance, the War of 1812, did Congress use its full-blooded power to make a declaration of war. In 1846 with Mexico, in 1898 with Spain, in 1917 and 1941 in the two World Wars, Congress simply recognized that a war did in fact exist. In addition there have been over 150 occasions (161 were listed by the Library of Congress in 1970) on which the United States has used armed force abroad without any congressional declaration of war, mainly under the President's authority (and obligation) to protect American life, property, and vital interests. Truman in 1950 involved the United States in a conflict in Korea (justified as a 'police action' under the auspices of the United Nations), which cost 33,000 American lives and nearly 160,000 American casualties, without any formal authorization by Congress at all. The long, steady, deepening involvement in Vietnam began as presidential 'defensive' action, followed by the Tonkin Gulf resolution of 1964, a congressional resolution which by-passed the issue of a declaration of war by authorizing the President 'to take all necessary measures. . . to prevent further aggression' and setting the whole affair in a context of response to an attack on U.S. naval vessels. From this developed an all-out but still undeclared war fought 'defensively' and extended, under the doctrine of 'hot pursuit', into Thailand, Laos, and Cambodia.

It was the hubristic excesses (and disasters) of the Vietnam war which impelled the nation to look afresh at the President's sweeping powers in foreign policy and war-making. The result was the passage of the War Powers Resolution in 1973 which obliged the President to report to Congress within forty-eight hours of committing armed forces abroad. The use of such forces would have to end within sixty days unless Congress authorized a longer period. A further thirty days' grace was permitted to ensure 'safe withdrawal.' What exactly is the Resolution's effect? Does it prevent future Vietnams? Johnson, after all, had 'reported,' however deceptively, to Congress in 1964 and 1965 and Congress had certainly given him an endorsement which, as he said, was like 'Grandma's nightdress': 'it covered everything.' Did the War Powers Resolution perhaps even enhance the President's power by authorizing 'sixty-day wars'?

Time alone can provide reliable answers to such questions, but the mere fact that they can be asked demonstrates once again the peculiarly exposed and ambiguous position of the Presidency. Expected, in a crisis, to do whatever is necessary, the President yet lacks for day-to-day purposes of government the kind of politico-constitutional radar that a parliamentary system can provide a responsive executive. He cannot get an advisory opinion from the courts; they will pronounce only after the deed. He cannot get a disinterested ruling from his Congress, and even to seek it is to run the risk of making a damaging admission of infirmity of purpose. He cannot get it from his party, since it no longer exists in a serious institutional form. He cannot get it from his Cabinet because it is a non-entity. He can only get it from his entourage in those very rare cases where there is a courtier honest and bold enough to tell the truth, however unpalatable; there are not many Roosevelts fortunate enough to have a Harry Hopkins. There remains only one sounding board disinterested and yet informed, politically sagacious but not committed to any single political cause. This is the press or, to be more comprehensive, the media.

The chart of relationships between American Presidents and the media is a long and fluctuating one, but, with allowances made for temporary divagations, it moves in only one direction, toward a greater, if not necessarily a more compatible, intimacy. In this as in so many other areas the Roosevelt era seems to be a watershed. The New Deal's impact on everybody, the new type of leadership that Roosevelt provided, the inadequacies of Congress and congressional Democrats in particular as intermediaries in this process—all combined to direct Roosevelt's attention to the potentialities for influence that the media offered, particularly the new medium of broadcasting. For the first time a President could appeal to the electorate personally, in their own homes, by the device of the 'fireside chat,' informal, unforceful, but oh how insidious! All intermediaries, constitutional or institutional, were bypassed. The people's leader spoke directly to his flock. Moreover, by the regularity and intimacy of his weekly press conferences and the network of White House—press liaisons that his aides maintained, Roosevelt was able to use the press as his eyes and ears, antennae that could reach beyond White House and Capitol Hill to tell him what the readers of that press were thinking.

Since Roosevelt there has been progress, if that is the word, in only one direction. No President, with the marginal exception of Kennedy, has had an equally deft and delicate relationship with the press corps, combining ability to play on that extremely fine-tuned instrument with an ear sensitive enough to catch accurately the echoes that rebound from it. The temptation, always latent, which indeed Roosevelt himself did not always resist, is to treat the press merely as something to be manipulated. The coming of television has intensified this.

The ability to put one's image, 'in living colour,' even if so far in only two dimensions, into the voter's living room has acted on Presidents like a wonder drug on athletes. They fear its consequences but cannot resist its potentialities. The superficialities of appearance count far more than ever; the message is in permanent risk of being subordinated to the medium. In a country where virtually all television is commercial it brings with it to a degree that even the most crassly commercial of newspapers never did the values of the market-place. The calculations of politics become the higher mathematics of market research. The fact that nothing can be conclusively proved about the reliability of such research has not prevented its gurus acquiring an ascendancy in the planning of campaigns and the presentation of policies which far exceeds the grubby influences exerted on the White House by the potential bosses of yore. Moreover the intrinsic costliness of the medium has, as we have seen, added enormously to the expense of campaigning, with far-reaching implications for the democratic ideal of making the processes of politics open to all.

Worst of all, though, is the intrinsically one-way nature of the medium. A Roosevelt 'manipulating' the press is still a human being talking to and, at least in some measure, obliged to listen to a *corps d'elite* of political observers who do more than reproduce their master's voice. They analyse it, comment on it, criticize it. It is going too far, as some enthusiasts have done, to equate the presidential press conference, even in its heyday, with Question Time in the House of Commons. Even the boldest of journalists is not an adequate sparring partner for the elected tribune of the sovereign people, and where the President is one and the press corps are many most of the advantages of manoeuvre lie with him. But with appropriate allowances made, the Washington press corps, which for knowledgeability and assiduity has no equal in the world, does fill a gap which as we have seen threatens seriously to impair the healthy functioning of the Presidency. Both collectively and sometimes individually, as in the instances of influential journals like the *New York Times* and the *Washington Post,* the press is a power in its own right, something which a President can no more ignore than the rival organs of government. It constitutes, without doubt, an establishment, and, like all establishments, it has its tastes and its biases. It has obvious other weaknesses, the commercialism and pomposity of some of its proprietors, and the vanity and pretentiousness of some of its prima donnas; but, despite increasing concentrations of ownership, it still reflects the genuine diversity of America, and despite the tireless seductions of those who seek its favours it still preserves a high professional integrity. What it would mean to American institutions, and especially to the modern Presidency, if these qualities were lost, can readily be imagined if one tries to envisage Watergate without the exposures that blew it skyhigh.

Unfortunately television, not because of any lack of integrity or courage by individual reporters or teams, but by the essential nature of the medium, is incapable of doing an analogous job, while the temptations which it offers to a President without scruples are only too obvious. It was no accident that Nixon in 1972 campaigned almost entirely on TV or that during his Presidencies he held far fewer press conferences than any other President of modern times. Obviously no President, and no democracy, is going to dispense with the facility that television affords of presenting the image of the ruler directly to the ruled. Nor should it be impossible to control and limit the advantages that this, left to itself, must confer on the incumbent as against his critics. What no regulations or controls can do is to protect the monarch from the image of himself, from the isolation of the man in the studio, from the illusion that because he speaks to millions and is seen by millions he is therefore truly representing them. In this sense television heightens the burdens on the President by insulating him still further from reality. It leaves him with his central problem, of communication, further from solution than ever, because that problem is not the problem of communicating to, but of receiving communications from the multiple groups and entities that make up the country he has to lead. Without a firm party base, without an easy or regular dialogue with the legislature, without near-equals in Cabinet, the President is more nearly insulated in the second half of the twentieth century than at any previous period in American history. How to overcome this, while still preserving the proper prerogatives of his office, is the central problem for the modern President.

NOTES

1. Why, one may ask, has voting turnout declined since television became an integral part of presidential campaigning?

2. Eisenhower's illness stimulated efforts to make legal provision for Presidential incapacity and in 1967 the twenty-fifth Amendment was ratified providing two methods by which the Vice-President can become Acting President: (a) if the President, in writing, informs Congress of his own incapacity, or (b) if the Vice-President and a majority of the Cabinet or of some 'other body' created by Congress pronounces him so.

CHAPTER 3

THE AMERICAN PRESIDENCY: A GERMAN PERSPECTIVE

Margarita Mathiopoulos

Perhaps it was only "leftist humor"; certainly it was a sign of the times. After the Bundestag made its final decision in November 1983 to deploy American Pershing II and cruise missiles, a backbencher of the Social Democratic Party (SPD) stood in the lobby of the Parliament and compared President Reagan and his administration with Adolf Hitler. Similar sentiments were repeated in November 1984 at a demonstration for Nicaragua in West Germany's capital of Bonn. The Protestant theologian Helmut Gollwitzer from Berlin placed Ronald Reagan in the same class as Hitler, Stalin and Pinochet.[1] Similarly, it may have been only a careless reflex which prompted a highly placed official of the Christian Democratic Union (CDU) and member of the government coalition to "leak" his opinion that German re-unification was inevitable. The leak followed Italian Foreign Minister Giulio Andreotti's description of the Federal Republic's diplomacy towards East Germany as a Pan-Germanistic vision. It is probably also only a passing variation of "German McCarthyism" that in certain journalistic and intellectual circles one may be jokingly "uncovered" as a CIA agent for daring to make positive comments about America.

This newly awakened anti-Americanism of both the Left and Right has led Germany's European neighbors and its American allies to become more interested, and even concerned, about the new political culture of Germany.[2] There has been a growing movement towards the Green-National Neutralism and Pacifism, an emphasis on German interests, and efforts to form a new *Ostpolitik* within the context of an inner-German consensus. In addition, there has been a remarkable search for a specifically German historical-political identity.

Are these symptoms evidence of the creation of a new German national consciousness? Or are they merely the expression of the current phase of the German *Zeitgeist,* which was always rather receptive to irrational strains? An American expert on Germany, John Vinocur, has been critical of the growing "German Malaise." He sees a tendency for the Green and alternative movements to separate themselves from the 30 year long German-American community of values. In his article "Europe's Intellectuals and American Power," Vinocur concludes that "following the lead of Gunter Grass, pop political writers in West Germany depict the U.S. as an oafish bully from which Germany must keep their distance.[3] This describes only a section of the wide spectrum of public opinion in the Federal Republic. Despite all the "German-American Irritations," the German Federal Republic (GFR), and in particular the ruling Christian-Liberal coalition, remains the most politically and militarily loyal, and the economically strongest European partner of the United States.[4]

The Federal Republic has been in transition since the beginning of the 1980s. This is demonstrated by changes in the historical, political and social self-perception of the Germans. The German vacillations ("deutsche Wechselbäder") have implications for German-American, German-Soviet, German-European and inner-German relations. The classical East-West conflict, which set the limits for German policy, may be moving towards a new dimension since Bonn began its struggle towards "emancipation." This new German political culture, at best, might be a passing West-West dissonance, at worst, it could lead to the dissolution of the Alliance.

The history of anti-American tendencies in Germany illuminates the relationship of the Federal Republic with the United States and the American presidency. A backward glance at these anti-American intellectual trends indicates their roots in an ignorance characteristic of the German idealism and romanticism from Hegel to today's Green cultural pessimism. Phases of harmony and turbulence in West German-American relations since the Second World War are briefly outlined as well as the decisive factors leading to continuity and change in German public opinion towards the US and the American presidency. In addition, the Federal Republic's evaluation of America's *Deutschlandpolitik* from the Fifties to the Eighties is analyzed as well as the influence of the German Chancellors from Adenauer to Kohl over Germany's *Amerika-Bild*.

Historical Misunderstandings: From German Idealism to the Green Cultural Pessimism

"Ladies and gentlemen, German-American friendship is based on the German contribution to America's development, on America's help after the Second World War. . . .[5] With this statement, President Karl Carstens ended his speech before both houses of Congress on October 5, 1983. The speech marked the Tricentennial Anniversary of German settlement in America. The German immigration into the New World began with 13 families from Krefeld who landed in Philadelphia on October 6, 1683. Seven million Germans followed. Many of them wanted to escape the economic and social shackles of the Old World. They wished to build a freer and more tolerant society on the other side of the Atlantic. As farmers and merchants, as soldiers and teachers, as politicians, scientists, and artists, German immigrants contributed greatly to the flourishing of the United States. These immigrants became and wanted to become Americans. They *voluntarily* left Europe and assimilated themselves just as *voluntarily* into the political, economic and social culture of America. This potential for personal growth and development enabled immigrants to contribute to the seemingly inexhaustible *élan vital* of American society. President Regan described this unique cultural-political experiment in the following words: "The United States is a nation of great size and many resources, but our richest resource is our people. They are fiercely independent and. . . they cherish their liberty above all else. It is a place where the cultures of many nations have blended to produce one culture—that which we call 'American.' "[6]

Although fifty million Americans claim to be of German descent, these people understandably consider themselves to be one hundred percent American. They feel closer to American political and democratic traditions than to a German culture and history which they have never experienced. The annual Steuben Parade, the numerous German *Wursthäuser,* or the diverse "club-mania" for the preservation of German culture and tradition, demonstrate fondness for nostalgic memories and not the influence of a German lobby in Washington. German-Americans had virtually no influence on the German *Amerika-Bild* as demonstrated by the misconceptions and ignorance about the American political system displayed by the scholars, poets, and politicians who stayed behind in Germany. Of course, Americans of German descent, from General Steuben to Henry Kissinger, have actively shaped the political culture of the United States. But didn't they act in the name of American and not German interests?[7]

The purpose here is not to disavow the 300 years of friendly German-American relations. Rather it is to recognize that the expectations attached to them have been too high. In this way both sides can avoid disappointments and misunderstandings.

Disappointments and misunderstandings have developed partly because of the different impact of historical events. One major difference was in the national development of Germany and that of the United States. The Enlightenment, for instance, affected Germany and America in fundamentally different ways. In America, the impetus for the Enlightenment was a pragmatically oriented political movement and resulted in the establishment of a constitution based on the principle of the sovereignty of the people. Its impetus in Germany was based on moral-philosophical postulates and resulted in the strengthening of the existing authoritarian structures. In addition, the intellectual and political leaders of America were eminently practical people who wanted to create a new commonwealth; they considered ideas as tools to realize their goals of freedom and democracy. Nothing comparable occurred in Germany. The concepts of a social contract and popular sovereignty which were characteristic of the Enlightenment in the West, did not develop a wide following in Germany. The impetus of the movement was diverted to questions concerning morality and self-realization.

The Enlightenment's decline in Germany and the subsequent predominance of a Herderian cultural nationalism and a pessimistic romanticism favored a view of humanity diametrically opposed to the American one. Germans tended to conceive of individuality not in pragmatic, political, and egalitarian but in mystical and metaphysical terms. It can be understood as "a special, physical manifestation in which the holy spirit reveals itself from time to time, be it in the form of individual persons or in communal institutions."[8]

Under these circumstances it is understandable that the New World remained closed to a large part of German thought and German thought remained closed to the Americans. Ernst Troeltsch once wrote that anyone who believes in natural rights, in the equality of people, and that a complete union of the two is an ostensible goal worth striving for must, for better or worse, recognize in German romantic idealism and nationalism a mixture of mysticism and brutality. On the other hand, whoever views the historical process as a progressive realization of God's will that is reflected in the national spirit and as a synthesis of national individualities that can only develop their full potential in competition with each other, can see in the western Enlightenment nothing but a vulgar rationalism and an atomistic egalitarianism, a mixture of bad taste and pharisaism.[9]

The "closing out" or "rejection" of the United States as an expression of conscious historical development and the social "suppression" of

Americanism manifested itself in Hegel's "Lectures on the Philsophy of History" in the Winter Semester of 1882: "After we have put aside the New World and the dreams that can be attached to it, we go over to the Old World, i.e. to the arena of world history." This type of "suppression"—a cause of later anti-Americanism—is a common thread woven through the German spirit (Befindlichkeit). In almost all scholarly and political circles of the nineteenth century all too often there reigned the consensus that on the other side of the Atlantic a "civilization of barbarians" chased after dollars to the beat of negro music while stepping over corpses and without giving a hoot about intellect or culture.

Americans had created a society of rabble (Gleichheitsflegel) in their haste to achieve social equality for all according to Heinrich Heine, who complained in 1840 of "the frightful prison of freedom, where. . . the most loathsome of all tyrants—the masses—practices its crude reign." This complacent arrogance and the ignorant juxtaposition of German "Kultur" with American "barbarism" seemed inexhaustibly abundant. Instead of criticizing themselves, the Europeans turned to America. Apparently as a reaction to European dissatisfaction, a mood began to spread in 1855 which borrowed its name from Ferdinand Kürnberger's book "American-Fatigue" (Amerika-Müde).

The undisputed center of the world, Europe, and especially Germany, nursed animosities that wavered between envy, insecurity and fear. Thus, Nikolaus Lenau, himself an immigrant, dismissed the American spirit as simply the "businessman's soul." For Hebbel the Americans were "lacking poetry," for Schopenhauer they were "lowly utilitarians," for Nietzsche "peculiarly spiritless," and for Jacob Burckhardt "mere business." For Thomas Mann, who had witnessed America first hand, they were "racketeers and entrepreneurs," and for the re-emigrant Karl Zuckmayer they were "without tradition and culture."[10] It was not specific criticisms of American failures, but general and arrogant intellectual mistrust.

During the Weimar Republic this theme fluctuated between the "decadent soul" of the Americans postulated on the Right, and the optimism of Wilsonian politics on the Left.[11] The anti-Americanism of German conservatism was apparent in the German intellectual community's comparison of German *Kultur* with western civilization, and of German spirituality with the Anglo-Saxon business mentality. The revolutionary Right of the Weimar Republic and the reactionary conservatives of the *Kaiserrech* demonized an imaged cultural and economic mass-Americanism. The revolutionary Left equated the United States with capitalism and imperialism. Finally, the intellectual propagandists of the National-Socialist movement appropriated the whole spectrum of anti-Americanism, and integrated the previously dispersed prejudices about American government, culture and economics. Thus arose a complete and negative representation of the "measureless and decadent continent."[12]

The more German thought both mysticized and rejected the American economic-technical process, the more unprepared it was to understand the deeply rooted tradition that lay beneath an apparent surface of hypermodernity. The more Germany dismissed as mere "accumulation" what was in reality both the preservation and further development of a pluralistic national and social order, the more Germany was unable to recognize that the creation of a "total state" in Germany had to stand in fundamental opposition to the democracy of the United States. Because German public opinion during the Weimar Republic misjudged the United States and refused to recognize America as a compass which could lead the way out of Germany's own internal systemic crisis, the reaction of the US towards the Third Reich remained incomprehensible.

Adolf Hitler hated Franklin Roosevelt more fanatically than any other statesman because Roosevelt exposed the fallacies of Hitler's thesis that economic crisis could only be surmounted through dictatorship. Hitler expressed his opinion of the American "system" in these terms: "These are the final death throes of an out-dated and corrupt system that is a shame for the history of its people. Since the Civil War, which the South lost despite all historical logic and all spiritual health, the Americans have found themselves in a realm of political and popular decay. It was not merely the South that was defeated but the American people themselves. Under the superficial cover of rising economic and political power, America has since been pulled into the whirl of progressive self-destruction." Hitler was sure, however, that "the healthy elements of the United States will one day awake, . . . that the call of National Socialism will free the American people from their ruling clique and once more give them the chance to become a great nation."[13]

With the increasing radicalization of the National Socialist movement, the tendency to view the American government as the antipode of the Nazi regime increased. It is therefore no surprise that American popular opinion and parts of Congress reacted almost indifferently to the dramatic events in Germany for a full decade. Attempts like that of the Dickstein Committee to convince America to give up its isolationism remained unsuccessful for years. Not until President Roosevelt's renowned Quarantine Speech in 1937 did the American Administration's foreign policies begin to change.

It is interesting to remember that in postwar more attention was given to the partial failure of the New Deal than to its long lasting effects. For a long time the Germans did not recognize the achievements of the reformer Franklin D. Roosevelt; instead they were convinced of Roosevelt's "betrayal" in his role as wartime President. German revisionists of both the Left and Right have contributed to these ambiguous sentiments concerning the Roosevelt Presidency.[14] As long as the mention of the names of Wilson and Roosevelt evokes only harsh memories of "Versailles" and "Yalta," a shadow of history will always fall across German-American relations.

The division of Germany after World War II introduced a new era in German-American relations, which the Germans however only fully recognized after three decades of changing self-perception. From the 1950s through the end of the 1980s the political dialogue between the Federal Republic and the United States remained more or less homogeneous. The relationship with America did not turn delicate until the early 1980s, when national security policy became a mass issue. The "peace movement" and the Greens no longer leave thoughts of German reunification to "reactionary" dreamers but "guiltily" suggest that anti-Americanism and the idea of a unified Germany are connected. Their unsettling and unreflecting yearning for a safe, pure, anti-modern, anti-Western, and "homey" ("heimatvolel") world should be viewed as an expression of a new German cultural pessimism and nationalism. Where is the Federal Republic heading?

The Fifties under Adenauer (1949-1963): "America, hipp, hipp, hurrah!"

"Maybe one can only understand what one loves." A sober analysis will reveal that the relationship between the Germans and the Americans after the Second World War actually developed on the basis of mutual ideological affinity which was taken for granted, and American economic generosity. One can hardly speak of a mutual affection. Who liked the Germans after the war? They did not even like themselves after all that had happened. How could they possibly approach others self-confidently and with an open mind?

Germany found itself in a political dilemma after 1945 which had long-term national and international consequences. It was split by a historical discontinuity; its recent past was filled with suffering, its presents confronted Germany with national division, and its future appeared to have already been determined by these two factors.

The newly created Federal Republic had the traumatic task to forge both a new political establishment and a constitutional framework. At the same time, the new state was to have a limited and provisional political status, a "Transitorium" as Theodor Heuss called it, a transitory stage on the path to a reunified Germany. On the one hand, under this consciously cultivated provisionality, West Germany did not wish and could not develop a historical consciousness. On the other hand, the establishment of a political consensus for the Federal Republic had to be accomplished despite the openness of the German question, despite the suppression of Germany's past and the difficulty of accepting the contemporary historical perspective, and despite the postponement of a German identity until some hypothetical day X of national unity.

The vacillation between denial and acceptance of history, between plaintive self-abnegation and constructive assessments contributing to a new democratic identification was compensated by Konrad Adenauer's decision to integrate Germany with the West. The latent political and social problems inherent in Germany's unanswered national question were balanced by a bipartisan ideological consensus of the miracle of Germany's economic policies until the student revolts of the 1960s.

The division of Germany was, from the beginning, the center of the Federal Republic's political focus. Indeed, under the strict formula of the Hallstein Doctrine, a nation's status with the FRG was automatically defined as either "good," "bad," or "unexistent" until the end of the 1960s. This inordinately difficult condition automatically affected the Federal Republic's relations to all other nations, and in particular to the protecting power, namely, America. West Germany's foreign policy was also determined by the state of US-Soviet relations.

The post-war psychological reaction of West German society towards the United States was complex. Germans showed the emotional reflexes of a conquered people, though these ranged from indifferent passivity to defiance of the "enemy." Goebbels' propaganda, which had emphasized the horrors of the American carpet bombing as well as the Morgenthau Plan, had a lasting effect and gave Germans a distorted picture of the conquering Americans. This image was supported by the early American occupation policies, which officially followed the main lines of the Morgenthau Plan. De-nazification and re-education were felt by the Germans to be instruments used to humble and weaken their country.[15]

The first Berlin crisis of 1948 was the decisive turning point in the political and psychological relationship between the American conquerors and the conquered Germany. At the end of March 1948, the Soviets restricted access to Berlin. After the three Western Allies introduced a currency reform for their zones in Germany and Berlin, the Soviets escalated their action to a total blockade. The Americans responded forcibly to this cold war confrontation with a massive airlift to supply and rescue the city. It was President Truman's determination to save Berlin despite strong Soviet pressure that created a new foundation of trust between Germans and Americans. The Americans now appeared as saviors who helped create the foundation for the new German state in 1949, the Federal Republic of Germany.

Konrad Adenauer had an incredibly convincing manner, which he effectively used to build and shape his image as the trustworthy father-figure of the West-German State among the German people, with sentences such as: "In the states of the western part of Germany there is a natural longing to rise out of the limited boundaries of nationality towards the fulfillment of a European consciousness."[16] Adenauer was able to create and maintain the image of a solid, and dependable alliance partner for both the Europeans and Americans for over a decade.

Adenauer's political accomplishments included giving a broken people their spirit back and binding these people to the West. He established a democratic-pluralistic political system, where just a short time before a totalitarian regime had been practicing its abuses. He built up trust among the German people for the United States and the *Deutschland-politik* of the President. Adenauer set in motion, with American help, an economic prosperity never before experienced. Not even future extreme crises could shake the foundations of the Federal Republic. Adenauer's policies were just as popular in the US as they were in Germany. President Eisenhower and the American people were very pleased with Germany, as Richard E. Neustadt later wrote.[17] Americans interpreted the German *Wirtschaftswunder* as a US success. In addition, Germany had become both an important trading partner as well as a significant area for US-investment. It was said that Germany was one corner of the world where the United States could flourish. An American economist of German descent, Henry Wallich, later a member of the Federal Reserve Board, summarized the view of many Americans at the time: work is the German form of psychotherapy.

One of the disadvantages of West Germany's phenomenal initial success was that American expectations concerning German virtues rose to an unrealistically high level. The Federal Republic, a state with its own problems and interests, could not possibly fulfill them. From 1949 to 1963, Americans viewed the Federal Republic not only as an ally but also as a protege with which they identified psychologically. The Federal Republic was seen as an integral part of the American system, and that meant whoever hurt or injured Germany, injured America.[18]

During the Eisenhower era, German-American relations were better than ever before or after. The personal ties between John Foster Dulles and Konrad Adenauer molded German-American relations into an almost symbiotic structure. Adenauer welcomed advice from Dulles on almost all issues. The chancellor also had demonstrable influence on American foreign policy. For example, at the 1955 Geneva summit conference the Americans accepted Adenauer's formula of "no detente without progress in the German question." In addition, Adenauer and Dulles were united by a common anticommunist stance. One occasionally had the impression in the 1950s that the horrors of the Moscow regime were being used to ignore Germany's historical responsibility for the past. After all, it was the totalitarian Nazi Regime which enabled Soviet communism to establish itself in Europe and to divide Germany.

The mutual respect between Eisenhower, Dulles and Adenauer reflected the positive picture Germans had of America in the 1950s. At that time, over 70% of the Germans would have been prepared to go through hell or highwater with the Americans. In large part this was due to Adenauer's charisma and commanding personality, which influenced both the Germans' perception of themselves as well as their *Amerika-Bild*. Another factor was the young Republic's social, political, and economic consolidation and its successful integration into the Western alliance vis-a-vis the transplantation of a socio-political model based on American ideas and ideological beliefs. German public opinion, the press, and the few experts in American politics were mainly concerned with the American president's *Deutschlandpolitik* and retained a positive perception of America despite growing changes on the bilateral level.[19]

German-American relations began to shift almost imperceptibly when Khrushchev put pressure on Berlin between 1958 and 1961. The second Berlin crisis, resulting from his 1958 ultimatum, presented the US for the first time with the option of acting either in favor of detente or in the interest of its German *Bundesgenosse*. The friendship between Dulles and Adenauer only lasted one more year, when it became clear that Dulles placed greater priority on overall US goals in central Europe than on the interests of an allied statesman. Willy Brandt recalled in an April 1982 interview in the "Corriere della Sera" that Dulles had confided to him years before that, even though much separated American and Soviet policy, they had one thing in common—maintaining the division of Germany.

At the 1959 meeting of foreign ministers in Geneva, the GDR was to play the same role as the Federal Republic for the first time. The Herter Plan which foresaw free elections for the reunification of Germany had to take a back seat to a "mixed German committee," in which representatives from the GDR would take part, albeit not on an equal footing. In March, 1961, Averell Harriman, special Ambassador of President Kennedy, announced that the US would give up the negotiating positions taken in 1959 and 1960. He felt that all discussions about Berlin had to be started from scratch.

Adenauer viewed with great distrust the bilateral negotiations between Kennedy and Khrushchev in Camp David, as well as in Vienna in June, 1961. Bonn had the impression it was being consulted but not fully informed, and above all it felt that its interests were not being fully accepted. Kennedy's and Adenauer's differences became especially vivid when on August 13, 1961, the Soviet Union and East Germany suddenly instigated the third Berlin crisis with the building of the wall. The Americans considered negotiations with the East reasonable and necessary to defuse the situation. The Germans, however, thought that any negotiations with the GDR would make the division of Germany more permanent.

Finally, the exchange of letters between Kennedy and Khrushchev beginning in September, 1961, thoroughly irritated Bonn. This episode—the first real "crisis of trust"—illustrated Bonn's sensitivity to all questions dealing with the other Germany. During the Adenauer era, the Americans conducted *Deutschlandpolitik*, while the Germans could only passively follow.

As John F. Kennedy—now a symbol and idol of several generations—travelled to the Federal Republic in June, 1963, he was welcomed as a hero. Driving in an open car through the streets of Bonn and Berlin, Kennedy was cheered by crowds who saw him as a champion of the people. Kennedy was so overwhelmed by this demonstration that he remarked to one of his aides, if any future president ever feels discouraged, just tell him: "Go to Germany." Twenty years later, in June 1982, Kennedy's statement had lost its meaning when President Reagan was met in Germany by riots, squadrons of police, and anti-Reagan slogans.

Kennedy's legendary statement: "Ich bin ein Berliner" was a sign of America's determination to keep West Berlin. However, his speech at *Pauls-kirche* marked a turning point for German-American relations for the 1960s. The message to Germany was clear: from now on, they could not count on American support for the type of reunification conceived of by Adenauer and Dulles. Then Kennedy endorsed a process begun in 1962 with the Cuban Missile Crisis and confirmed on June 10, 1963 in his American University address: namely, the pursuit of detente through direct negotiations with the Soviet Union.[20]

Omissions of German institutions during the 1950s might have contributed to repeated flare-ups of anti-Americanism later on. First of all, it is puzzling that there is no monument of an American President in West Germany. One might think that President Roosevelt's commitment to free Europe during World War II would mark a pivotal event for the Germans, as well as Secretary of State Marshall's generous economic aid policy, or President Truman's determination to end the Berlin-Blockade. However, in Berlin, Hamburg, Munich, Cologne and Bonn, for example, the names Roosevelt, Truman, Eisenhower and Marshall do not appear, though each has Kennedy streets and bridges. America's youngest President seems to remain Germany's favorite, although he did less for German reunification than his three predecessors.

Another important, but often neglected factor was the creation of new professorships in political science at German universities, which were held by former emigrants to America and by America-experts. Their research not only helped to deepen German understanding of the American political system, but their studies comparing American self-perception and German political culture served also to portray America's democracy as a model for the FRG. However, political science is still disparaged by the German public and some academic circles don't even recognize it as a discipline. Whereas political science in Anglo-Saxon tradition is especially respected—and this must have something to do with democratic parliamentary history—the German attitude toward this field reflects their unhappy historical experience with authoritarian political structures.[21]

If an idealization of American political culture and ideology spread through Germany during the 1950s, this was not part of a historical friendship between two countries, nor was it evidence of a sound knowledge of America's open society. Rather, it was an expression of deep gratitude towards a nation which had raised Germany up out of its ruins and generously helped it build a new political democracy and free market economy. West Germany welcomed its membership in NATO primarily for political, military and practical economic reasons. However, the third fundamental element of NATO-philosophy—the formative consensus of a cultural and ideological interdependence among the West, and the commitment to a common liberal tradition—was neglected.

The Sixties under Erhard and Kiesinger (1963-1969): "Amis raus aus Vietnam", but stay in Germany

During the 1960s the German *Amerika-Bild* moved slowly towards an emotional polarization which was to reawaken traditional clichés. Whereas strong pro-Americanism (Hurra-Amerikanismus) had thrived with uncritical support for American foreign policy and model of development, the superpower's movement towards detente and the American involvement in Vietnam confused many Germans. Neutralist and pro-communist movements crystalized and protested against the *Bonner System* and its "establishment." This newly formed left-wing anti-Americanism was motivated by self-critical debate within the United States on its role as a world power. This merciless internal debate about the war in Vietnam astonished and pleased the German political establishment, who after the Second World War could only discuss their own history with great difficulty.

The newly formed German Left gathered around authors with an anti-American reputation, like Leo L. Matthias and Reinhard Lettau. Anti-American publications of the German right-wing had neglible influence. One must obviously not confuse the anti-Americanism of the left-wing student revolts in West Germany and elsewhere with the broad public opinion of the Germans in the 1960s, who continued to view the United States as a solid partner.

In Washington and Bonn two politicians came into office at the end of 1963: Lyndon B. Johnson and Ludwig Erhard. They seemed to understand each other perfectly. "Relations with Germany would surely be close in this administration, US-observers soon agreed."[22] Despite the friendly ties between President Johnson ("I like simply everything about him)" and Chancellor Erhard ("I love President Johnson, and he loves me"), American support could not prevent the German Chancellor and "Father of the Economic Miracle" from being forced to resign at the end of 1966.

During the Erhard era the development of international relations was marked by a striking paradox: On the one hand America was fighting the East by proxy in Vietnam, and on the other hand, continued extensive East-West negotiations. Bonn tried to come to terms with this new climate. The goal was to have as close relations with Washington as possible. Erhard's transatlantic efforts were continuously under attack. Former Chancellor Adenauer, Franz Josef Strauss, and Baron von Guttenberg constantly criticized the new Bonn course. This group of "German Gaullists" also condemned the MLF Project as an arrangement that would give Germany only the appearance of a voice in NATO nuclear policy, and thereby forcing Erhard and his "Atlanticist" colleagues into the defensive. Disputes with the FDP coalition partner on economic questions further weakened Erhard.

A critical German commentator described the end of the Erhard era: Bonn was not capable of winning any political capital out of its change of policy towards Washington. After the French-German treaty the FRG Government took great efforts to foster close ties with Washington, but the hope for special relations did not materialize. Despite constant confessions of Atlantic partnership; despite German support for American policies in China, Vietnam, and Santo Domingo; and despite the obligations for extensive arms purchases, these efforts remained unrewarded. The MLF, in 1963 still a concrete project, died, for which not only the Americans can be blamed, and the issue of American troop stationing in Germany, which had been latent since 1960, suddenly became acute when in April 1966, America withdrew 15,000 soldiers.[23]

Erhard's visit to Washington in late September 1966, signaled the beginning of the end of his term in office. The Chancellor floundered on the problem of offset costs, which had become a domestic question of prestige to the leaders of both countries. Despite warnings from both the German and American sides, Erhard just would not believe that "his friend Johnson" was not able to simply overlook the three billion dollars, owed by the FRG. George von Lilienfeld wrote: "His visit to Washington with its unpleasant end at Cape Kennedy was the most unenjoyable meeting that I have ever experienced in over 12 years of official contacts with the USA."[24]

Erhard's trip to the US also caused negative domestic reaction. The pro-French "gang" gained in strength, even though Jean Monnet assured the American Ambassador in Bonn, George McGhee, "they will find that de Gaulle has nothing to offer—that this is dead end."[25] In addition Erhard finally lost the support of German industry. As was reported in American diplomatic circles the patron of German economy, Kurt Birrenbach, confided to Jean Monnet, "German big business interests have decided to withdraw their support from Erhard, (which) would explain the generally non-cooperative attitude of the *Bundesbank* on the offset-problem. Industrial circles with an influence on the bank may be urging a hard line in the expectation that this would bring about Erhard's fall.'' Working in the same direction were the conspiratorial efforts of the former Finance Minister, and Adenauer's favorite for Chancellor, Etzel, who mobilized the "Ruhr industrailists" against Ludwig Erhard and thereby helped to prepare his fall.[26]

The Chancellor's visit to Washington also brought out additional aspects of German-American relations which were critical for German foreign policy. France's withdrawal from the military sector of NATO gave the Federal Republic more transatlantic influence, but "Germany is," in the words of Walt W. Rostow, "located astride the balance of power in Europe. . . . From the Communist point of view, in the pursuit of world power Germany remains the greatest possible prize."[27] A Senator confided to Marion Dönhoff in "Die Zeit" in July 1966, ". . . we know only too well that it is the Russians alone who have control over what the Germans so dearly want. DeGaulle may anger us, but he will never betray us—after all, we fought side by side in two World Wars."[28] This kind of irritation was expressed during Erhard's Washington trip in discussions with Secretary of State Rusk and President Johnson.

One key question which occupied Erhard and Schröder was "how to obtain a total nuclear strategy for the Alliance as a believable deterrent" for German public opinion. "In this direction German government policy needed some support. There were many influential people, if not in the administration then certainly in Parliament, that are unhappy with the current state of affairs and are looking for more or less strong alternatives or changes in the status quo. Sure, in the same breath they will declare they needed the U.S., would remain loyal to the U.S., etc., but in reality they were also looking in new directions; some solid arguments were needed before the German people in order to reassure them," of American determination—after the U.S. withdrew troops in tandem with the introduction of the policy of "flexible response"—to defend the Federal Republic when the chips were down. "The relative security felt by the people during the period of 'massive retaliation' when nobody even criticized extra expenses on the defense sector" was, as Erhard explained, no longer "felt since the introduction of the 'flexible response' strategy with its 'thresholds' and 'pauses.' "

Fears about nuclear strategy were voiced by Chancellor Erhard as early as the Sixties:

"Should the Russians for example want to take Hamburg, the FRG might reply with tactical nuclear weapons. The Soviets might answer with tactical nuclear weapons first also and might attack at

another point. Would at this point, or a little later, the decision to
employ a full response be made any easier for the US President
with the fires of war already on the world's horizons? To us, you
and the Russians, a big nuclear war is unthinkable as a solution.
But then how believable is our strategy of deterrence to the man in
the street in Germany? As long as there was the strategy of full
response and sure retaliation it sounded believable. With all our
trust in the US and our allies will we and the man in the street be
sure the rest of the world would be ready to die for the sake of saving Germany? These are very realistic fears disturbing the German
people.''

Foreign Minister Schröder argued in the same direction, ''that it is exactly because of this why the presence of US troops was so important as a
symbol of US involvement and a token and pledge of commitment. To
me, frankly, the thesis of 'massive retaliation' never made any military
sense but sounded just like a political argument that was convenient.''

The Americans tried to reassure the Germans. Dean Rusk told the
Chancellor, ''that the US had never abandoned any of the territory of its
Allies and taken enormous casualties to honor their commitments. They
had 7000 warheads in Europe they would certainly not abandon to the
Russians, and the only way the Russians could get them is 'to have them
stuffed down their throat.' '' Nevertheless Erhard was quite disturbed by
the American-Soviet non-proliferation talks ''to which the FRG could
fall victim not having even a voice in nuclear defense.''[29] A week later
Ambassador Averell Harriman gave an analysis of these questions in his
October 3, 1966 memorandum to the President and the Secretary of
State:

''Regardless of how we assess developments in Germany in the
years ahead, I am convinced that the Soviet leaders are deeply concerned over a possible reemergence of a German threat to Russian
security. The Kremlin desires a nuclear non-proliferation pact with
Germany particularly in mind. I seriously doubt that the Soviet
Union will be satisfied with a formula which would permit 'hardware participation' by the Germans. A possible quid pro quo for
Moscow's action in Southeast Asia would be our abandoning the
hardware option in our proposals for the pact. . . . In addition, a
mutual reduction in forces in Germany would probably appeal to
Moscow. . . . I recognize the political difficulties in Germany at
the present time, but our interests are so overwhelming to get the

war over in Vietnam, that I cannot help but feel we should move as rapidly as feasible."[30]

In his September meeting with the Chancellor, President Johnson had tried to no avail to dispel the German nuclear fears.

New frontiers were on the horizon—the Federal Republic's *Deutschlandpolitik* began to follow a more flexible path. The slogan of the 1960s was: progress in detente in pace with progress in the German question. The Americans welcomed and encouraged this change to realism which signified an increase in German acceptance of the European status quo.[31] Whereas in 1964 the Germans would not yield on the Oder-Neisse question—"these people are still victims of a false perspective, a perspective which may have had some validity a dozen years ago, but with each passing year becomes more unrealistic, and that they will in time see this"—"the Germans consider, wrongly I believe, that they have bargaining power toward reunification in the reunification of territories beyond the Oder-Neisse"[32]—Erhard confided to Johnson in his Washington visit that "few Germans still regard revision of Oder-Neisse line as sacred." The Chancellor confirmed that they were also trying to improve relations with other Eastern countries, especially Romania and Bulgaria. Finally, the softening of the Hallstein doctrine came through, although this still caused heated battles within the CDU.[33] In July 1966, Harriman recalled:

"I was opposed to the Hallstein doctrine. I was opposed to the idea that Adenauer developed—that the way to get unification of Germany was to be stubborn about everything and to refuse to accept the reality of the Soviet Zone of Germany—of course not recognition of East Germany. I felt, at that time, about the way Willy Brandt speaks today. . . . I thought we made a mistake in supporting this extreme policy. . . . and I thought we got too committed to the rigidities of Adenauer's views. Adenauer didn't really understand the Russians very well. But when he made his agreement of mutual recognition with Moscow, that broke the Hallstein doctrine, because he dealt with the principal, and having dealt with the principal, why should he refuse to deal with the other countries. . . . And today it's very much to our interest to pull Eastern Europe away from Moscow and I'm very glad to see the Germans trying to develop better relations with East Germany. The Hallstein doctrine has stood in the way. . . . We got too much involved in every detail of Adenauer's policies. . . . the manner in which we became so completely tied to the German policy didn't seem to me wise.''

As for the Russians, Harriman remembered, they had always been suspicious of the development of German *Ostpolitik* and the close German-American ties. "Now, the Russians do fear Germany. . . . Stalin did. He feared the future of Germany. . . . Khrushchev was afraid of the Germans. . . . I remember Khrushchev's telling me. I said, 'Why don't you accept the German situation, permit a united Germany? Why don't you develop a friendly basis?' He said, 'Well, they're revanchists.' And I said, 'That's ridiculous.' . . . And Khrushchev said, 'Oh, I know Adenauer would never engage in war.' He'd just called him a warmonger I think, but he said, 'I know Adenauer would never get into a war, but who do we know will succeed Adenauer—what their attitudes will be? What will be the attitude of Germany, if Strauss becomes the Chancellor?' . . . And today Kosygin—from my talks with him, I get the impression that they're not so afraid of the military might of Germany anymore because they are so preponderantly superior to them in nuclear power. But they don't want Germany to have anything to do with nuclear weapons. They're afraid of them. . . . They're afraid of their revanchist attitudes. But they're particularly fearful of our very close relations with the Germans, and fear that our policies may be influenced by the Germans, and if some incident happened, we might support Germany in some kind of activity which would be impossible for the Russians to accept. . . . But I feel, in dealing with the Germans, we're much better off to tell them the facts and tell them what our basic interests are. Then we can get along with them better. . . . Well, this is the spirit which I think is important to continue, because we don't want to have any element develop in Germany that doubts the stability of American alliance. That's the trouble. They're worried. They're concerned. They're a strong country."[34] From the beginning, Ambassador Harriman had not only grasped the subtleties and imponderables in German-American relations, but also encouraged a realistic and flexible approach toward *Ostpolitik* among German politicians.

The initiatives toward a new *Ostpolitik* begun in the Erhard period were now continued by the Grand Coalition (Grosse Koalition) under Kurt Georg Kiesinger and Willy Brandt.[35] Shortly after he became Chancellor, Kiesinger had his first talk with the American Ambassador, George McGhee, and assured him that "something new would happen." "The supreme German policy was not reunification but peace." Kiesinger's new course was based on the assumption "that we should *all together* try to achieve detente." The only difficulty he saw was that some Germans might believe that "the US would seek detente at the expense of reunification," or else as part of a "nuclear complicity" with the Soviet Union. "Germany should not put itself in the position of a girl who constantly seeks reassurance from an old lover 'that he still loves her.' "

The Chancellor also spoke about anti-American sentiment among Europeans, but he emphasized that "this was least true of all in Germany—despite efforts by the NPD (National Democratic Party of Germany) to stir it up."[36] Admittedly, the Left's anti-American demonstrations against the Vietnam War increased during the Kiesinger period. By 1968 there already more than half a million U.S. soldiers in Vietnam—not sufficient to halt communist gains in the South. The United States felt obliged to undertake more and more massive bombing missions in North Vietnam. In many circles within America as well as among the Europeans—whose official positions ranged from the outright condemnation of France to the unwilling support of England and increasing reluctance of Germany—the prevailing view as that the war would have to be ended by negotiation. In the US, the continually growing deficits, caused largely by military expenditures in Vietnam, led to calls for a reduction of military support for Europe as well as of US troop strength in the Federal Republic. The repeatedly-proposed Mansfield Amendment did worry the Germans, but as long as it was only a recommendation and a "fictional vision," not a binding decision, the German government took it in stride. The FRG was equally untroubled by the reduction of American troops in Europe from 366,000 in 1966 to just over 300,000 in 1968.

A new formula for the major issues in the future of the Alliance was set in 1967 in the Harmel Report, named after the Belgian Foreign Minister: NATO's double strategy was henceforth defined by guaranteeing the security of alliance members through military deterrence and by simultaneously striving for progress in the relaxation of East-West tensions. Military security and detente were no longer to be understood as mutually contradictory, but rather as complementary. This policy corresponded to American intentions to continue an arms-control dialogue with the Soviets as well as to the Bonn government's efforts toward a less strained relationship with its Eastern neighbors.[37] In theory, the Harmel Report is still part of NATO strategy, but in practice only Germans are still quoting it.

In early 1967 the Grand Coalition developed new guidelines toward the East, including for the first time a more conciliatory note toward Moscow, the Warsaw pact countries and the GDR.[38] Bonn of course still insisted that diplomatic recognition of East Germany was out of the question. Nevertheless, a change in mood was evident in a 1967 Chancellor Kiesinger letter addressed to his East German counterpart Willy Stoph as "Dear Mr. Prime Minister."[39] These words signified an indirect recognition of the statehood of the GDR. To be sure, Henry Kissinger caused some irritation in Bonn after his appointment as National Security Advisor under President Nixon. It became known that he had belonged to a study group of the United Nations Association of the United States who advocated full participation of both East and West Germany in their proposed European Security Council. But in the era of the Grand Coalition there was actually no reason to fear that either a Democratic or a Republican US-Administration would promote a "premature" diplomatic recognition of the GDR—something Bonn would view as contrary to German national interests.

Again, serious tensions in German-American relations beteen 1966 and 1969 were raised over the offset-costs, the exchange rate problem and in the non-proliferation treaty. When the Germans finally received the American-Soviet draft of the treaty for comment, Kiesinger called it an "atomic conspiracy," ex-Chancellor Adenauer in his last political statement compared it with an "inflated Morgenthau Plan," and Finance Minister Franz Josef Strauss called it "a new Versailles of cosmic dimensions." But the German fears were too hasty: as the Republican Richard Nixon entered the White House, the non-proliferation treaty was dropped from the American priority agenda; the Federal Republic was quietly handed the right to ratify the treaty only after satisfactory outcome of the negotiations on inspection rights between the International Atomic Energy Commission and Euratom.

The end of the Grand Coalition era occurred simultaneously with the end of Nixon's "era of automatic unity" between the United States and the Federal Republic. Supported by an overwhelming majority in the *Bundestag* (447 of the 496 seats), the Kiesinger/Brandt Coalition now approached Washington with new self-confidence. The self-assurance was echoed in a remark by a foreign policy advisor to the Chancellor: Germany must give up its self-denial of the Adenauer Era and replace it with a "deliberate, self-confident will towards independence."[40] A German commentator and American expert aptly characterized the predominant spirit:

". . . while the principle of alliance remains undisputed, its modalities are certain to come under close and critical scrutiny. . . . Germany is not about to take up a Gaullist attitude toward the United States. Opinion polls bear out the belief that America is still regarded as an indispensable and reliable partner. But the government of the Grand Coalition will no doubt take a more independent stance in defining Germany's national interest. The Federal Republic no longer feels like a ward of Washington. It will not hesitate to disagree with, and if necessary to deviate from, American-sponsored policies."[41]

The West German decision in December 1968, to hold the presidential election in West Berlin in March 1969—despite the Allies' advice against it—indicated a gradual crystalization of German self-confidence. Gustav Heinemann's election as President was a first signal for the coming Social-Liberal Coalition, which was also to venture a new phase in *Deutschlandpolitik*. A new era emerged in German-American relations: "From subservient client to independent partner."[42]

The Seventies under Brandt and Schmidt (1969-1982): (1969-1982): "Washington yes, but via Moscow"

Willy Brandt's inauguration as Chancellor in October 1969 was an important turning point in German history. Brandt, "Europe's Kennedy," personified the growing German self-consciousness which was already awakening during the CDU/SPD coalition. Brandt brought a Kennedy-like "compassion" to the Social-Liberal coalition. Even more so for foreigners than at home, Willy Brandt embodied "the other Germany," the "German conscience"; he was the symbol of the "democratic tradition" in Germany. For the first time since 1930 a Social Democrat was the head of government. For the first time in the 20 year history of the Federal Republic the CDU had been driven by an SPD/FDP coalition government into parliamentary opposition, in which it would stay for 13 years.[43]

A start towards new horizons and "New Frontiers," both in domestic and foreign policy, were Brandt's goals and visions, promises similar to those made by John F. Kennedy to America a decade before. Domestically, the new government planned economic and social reforms in order to provide the greatest number of citizens with social justice and a higher quality of life. In foreign policy, West Germany was to risk a new and open dialogue with the East. The Republic should transform and rejuvenate itself. Thus the primary focus of Brandt's policies were on an internal structural reorganization and a new definition and emphasis on *Ostpolitik*.[44].

Foreign relations were increasingly characterized by the newly won political latitude achieved by German-American cooperation in *Ostpolitik*. Willy Brandt took office at the same time as Richard Nixon, just as the "Era of Negotiation" and "Era of Detente" began. West Germany wanted to reshape its relations with the East and normalize its ties with the GDR; to accomplish this, it needed Western support. The United States wanted to reorganize East-West relations and add new and politically acceptable functions to its alliances, for which it needed, above all, the consent of the FRG. At the beginning Bonn and Washington were suspicious of each other, though later coordination between the two capitals on *Ostpolitik* functioned with remarkable smoothness. Successful German-American cooperation was more the result of common interests than a common strategy. Both Washington and Bonn won considerable operational flexibility in their foreign policies—America on a new global scale, the Federal Republic in Europe.[45]

The new American global strategy for detente was as follows: Just as in the 1940s when Roosevelt was able to contain Nazism with the aid of Stalin, Nixon and Kissinger now attempted to contain Russia with the help of the Chinese, a policy made possible through more relaxed relations with both nations. The containment of the geopolitical expansionism of the USSR was only possible through a change in Moscow's international behavior. This in turn, was only possible through detente, which was of use for both the United States and the Soviet Union. Nixon's and Kissinger's grandiose combination of a new Asian and East-West doctrine integrated into a global strategy of detente was a continuation of containment by other means.[46]

The new German concept of detente was naturally more modest: During the 1950s, Konrad Adenauer was able to contain the neutralist, Social-Democratic and right-wing reactionary political forces in the Federal Republic, by using political tactics and slogans which postponed the hoped-for German reunification until day X, and also quieted the fears of the FRG's Western allies by proclaiming absolute loyalty to the alliance. In a similar manner during the 1970s Brandt and Scheel were able to contain the intransigent right-wing reactionary forces in the CDU which opposed every concession to the East. Brandt's and Scheel's combination of German and American *Ostpolitik* and its use as a European strategy of detente created a more independent foreign policy role for the Federal Republic. For the first time since the war, German-German relations were not only taken up, but were also shaped by German actors themselves which meant a new substantive political quality for German affairs. From then on, the formula for *Deutschlandpolitik* was: Since detente is the basis for every step forward in the German question, we are prepared to make unilateral concession to achieve this prerequisite, and we agree that the solution to the German question will have to be postponed.

Brandt's new enthusiasm for *Ostpolitik* was viewed in Washington with some suspicion. Although the Chancellor and the President got along well with one another—"the meeting between Brandt and Nixon (April 1970) was surprisingly cordial, given the fact that neither man would have sought out the other's company, had not fate thrust the leadership of great nations upon them"[47]—German expert Henry Kissinger was nevertheless concerned about the long term effects of *Ostpolitik:*

> "It seemed to me that Brandt's new *Ostopolitik,* which looked to many like a progressive policy of quest for detente, could in less scrupulous hands turn into a new form of classic German nationalism. From Bismarck to Rapallo it was the essence of Germany's nationalist foreign policy to maneuver freely between East and West. . . . It should be remembered that in the 1950s, many Germans not only in the SPD under Schumacher but in conservative quarters traditionally fascinated with the East or enthralled by the vision of Germany as a 'bridge' between East and West, argued against Bonn's incorporation in Western institutions on the ground that it would forever seal Germany's division and preclude the restoration of an active German role in the East. This kind of debate about Germany's basic position could well recur in more divisive form, not only inflaming German domestic affairs but generating suspicions among Germany's Western associates as to its reliability as a partner."[48]

Ten years later, the remarks by the Americanized German Kissinger would ring like prophecy.

However, these detente agreements were overshadowed by the continuing Vietnam War. Presidential candidate McGovern's slogan "Come home America" expressed the desires of many Americans not only to reduce US troops in Germany, but to minimize American obligations throughout the world. The Young Socialists, who reached their political peak in the early 70s, unmistakably disapproved of the Americans' presence in Vietnam, as well as their continuing presence in Europe. There was still more evidence of an anti-American mood in Germany: public opinion pools revealed a pointed drop in German admiration of the US, and demonstrations protesting American maneuvers in the Nuremberg area were presented in the American media as proof of deeply rooted anti-American sentiments. In an interview published by an American magazine shortly before his visit to Washington in May 1973, the Chancellor defined a point of great importance to the German attitude towards America: "The so-called anti-Americanism arose out of exaggerations on this side of the ocean and a corresponding reaction over on your side."[49]

German-American relations during the Brandt era were marked by a paradoxical harmony. While their ideological temperaments were dissimilar, the Republican Nixon and the Social Democrat Brandt had been fated to a common political purpose. Each considered himself charged with a historical mission. Nixon formulated and practiced the beginnings of "a century of peace," ended the age of bipolar confrontation, the Cold War, and opened an era of negotiations with the Soviet Union and China—an era of mutual recognition and detente. Brandt's charisma helped him dare to attempt as many historical reparations as were politically achievable. The settlement of the Easter Treaties signified an important German step toward internal detente in Europe, opened up possibilities for a constructive German-German dialogue, and fulfilled a duty towards Poland and the USSR which had stood open since the end of World War II. Willy Brandt deeply impressed the entire world; he had brought the Germans one step closer to historic rehabilitation, but for this his own countrymen were the least thankful. Both politicians, Richard Nixon and Willy Brandt, experienced great personal triumphs in their election victories in 1972. Both statesmen suffered political defeat in 1974: in Watergate and the Guillaume affair.

When Helmut Schmidt became Chancellor in 1974, the German image of America had already begun to crack: the media had brought the Vietnam War into almost every German living room. Watergate aroused nothing but criticism, but at the same time, a French President's acceptance of diamonds from a cruel dictator was considered merely a gentleman's *faux pas*.

A step-by-step deterioration of German-American relations began during the Schmidt era, and was not spared from the influence of changing international relations. The shift in the political, economic, military and geostrategic interests of the individual countries caused a simultaneous shift in their potential individual strengths within the world mosaic. This new political situation of the 70s was comprised of several factors: the rise of Germany and Japan to economic superpowers and competitors of the United States; the economic and energy crises which hit Europe particularly hard, and which brought the Persian Gulf countries new quality of power; and the German-French hegemonic endeavors within the European Community. The new state of affairs was further defined by the Soviet Union's military and geostrategic neo-expansionism into Africa and Afghanistan, as well as by America's loss of prestige through the Vietnam War, Watergate, and the hostage crisis in Iran.[50]

With the decline of the American political, economic and military power, there came a subtle turning point in the American attitude toward Europe, Germany and NATO. The Americans began to seek political, moral, economic and military support from their allies—to whom they had offered 30 years of protection. The Europeans were expected to agree to an expansion of Allied obligations in the Far East, Africa, and the Persian Gulf. Perception of NATO by Presidents Ford, Carter and Reagan slowly changed from a limited Allied Treaty for a specific geographical area to a view of a vague and unlimited duty to the Alliance in general, or else one of disappointment. In this respect, the Americans held rather high expectations of the Germans: in case of another flare-up in the Middle East crisis they were supposed to have air bases ready for American forces and to place German ships in the Persian Gulf. In addition, the Federal Republic was expected to comply with American moral gestures, such as the Olympic boycott after the Soviet invasion of Afghanistan.[51] The Americans also assumed that, because of Soviet expansion, Bonn would reduce its now flourishing trade with the Soviet Union. All of these expectations flowed into frustrations on both sides of the Atlantic. World-political, strategic turbulence and economic questions could no longer be treated separately from one another. Differences over the interpretation of detente between America and Europe—and especially between Washington and Bonn—became even more evident.

Helmut Schmidt was on principle against operating outside the borders of the Alliance. To send armed forces to areas far from Europe was beyond possible consideration. Equally unlikely for Schmidt was a German contribution to a Rapid Deployment Force for protection of the Gulf Region. On the other hand, Schmidt believed that partial responsibility for world politics had accrued to Bonn, and that as a result of this development he, as Chancellor, would have to play a decisive role as mediator between East and West.

During his term as Chancellor, Helmut Schmidt had the opportunity to come to agreement with four American Presidents. With Jimmy Carter, however, he could not or would not get along. His sharp criticisms of the United States contributed to a cooling off in German-American relations in a time when the international situation consisted of conflicts and crises and Allied solidarity had become the order of the day. The German-American talks over the various problem areas—the discussion of the neutron bomb, SALT II, the Soviet SS-20 missiles, and the introduction of the INF—proceeded very slowly. They were not at all in the spirit of a long-time bilateral cooperation, but rather like "a married couple, who have been married for 30 years, can't stand each other anymore, but because of firmly accepted loyalties cannot separate." This image is confirmed by Carter and Brzezinski, as well as by Cyrus Vance, in each of their memoirs.

The Americans had great difficulties with Helmut Schmidt. Carter wrote in his diary: "Helmut is strong, somewhat unstable. . . postures, and drones on, giving economic lessons when others are well aware of what he is saying . . . very popular in his own country.[52] Zbigniew Brzezinski, of whom Helmut Schmidt had often complained to Carter, also shared the President's opinion:

"If the president and I admired the same people, we also shared similar dislikes. Among them the Chancellor of Germany, Helmut Schmidt, took the undisputed first place. This need not have been the case, for Carter's initial attitude toward Schmidt was one of respect and even deference. He knew that Schmidt had a better grasp of world economics, not to speak of the advantage of having inherited from his predecessors a healthy domestic economy. I had known Schmidt for at least a decade and a half prior to my going to the White House, and I had briefed Carter on Schmidt, presenting a most attractive and favorable picture. Prior to their first meeting Carter was eager to learn from, and to work closely with, the German Chancellor. That attitude was unfortunately not reciprocated. Schmidt, almost from the very first encounter, adopted a patronizing attitude, mixed with less than persuasive protestations of friendship. Invariably there followed nasty behind-the-scenes gossip to sundry American and German journalists. . . (His) inability to keep his tongue under control soured American-German relations to an unprecedented degree and lent respectability to the increasing German propensity to be highly critical of the U.S. President and of U.S. policies more generally."[53]

It is certainly a pity that because of poor personal relations between Carter and Schmidt, the time-proved relations between the two countries fell into a process of increasing decay. Jimmy Carter complained, "These peristent criticisms, often highly publicized, helped to legitimize anti-American sentiments in Germany."[54]

Helmut Schmidt continuously attempted to constructively influence the dialogue between the two superpowers although the concept of "detente" had lost its original meaning for the Americans and was only embraced by the Germans and a few other Europeans. His attempts might have had greater chances if the relationship between Schmidt and Carter had been better. Schmidt's good relations with Breshnev, the continuation of Brandt's *Ostpolitik Change through rapprochement,* and the intensification of trade with Moscow, East Berlin and Warsaw Pact countries, were viewed in the White House with incomprehension as "Bonn's solitary path." Through his "shuttle diplomacy" with Moscow, the Chancellor wanted to document that the Federal Republic was not America's 51st state, that Germany would follow a politically more independent course, and that Washington would have to accept security *partnership with the East* as a new integral part of German foreign policy. The Schmidt era left its succeeding administration a burdensome inheritance in the area of German-American relations.

The Eighties under Kohl (1982-): Anti-Americanism or pro-Germanism?

The Kohl/Genscher Government implemented NATO's "double-track-decision," softened the growing transatlantic mistrust and generally improved German-American relations. Nevertheless, the Bonn administration was unable to eliminate the mistrust dating back to the Schmidt era and fueled by pacifistic and alternative movements and by the Green Party. These *altdeutsche* (old-fashioned German) neutralist currents were viewed both by the Reagan Administration and by part of the American public as a revival of German anti-Americanism.[55]

Undeniably, there are anti-American and anti-Reaganite sentiments within these movements. There are trends towards political and military neutralism in the Federal Republic, and towards an *equidistance* vis-a-vis Washington and Moscow. Nevertheless, the causes of this newly arisen German nationalism appear to lie deeper: "The period after World War II put us Germans into a deep sleep and had a profound effect on our awareness of history."[56] The current resurgence of political controversy about the German question and Germany's attempts to accept its past stems from the abnormal German historical process after World War II. It is quite probably that the rise of the Green and alternative movement, which are on the search for a German identity, a German-German consensus and a definition of *Heimat* and patriotism, is a consequence of Germany's unrecognized recent history and of a deficit in self-assurance. The new anti-American and anti-Western *Weltanschauung* can be seen as a relic from a difficult past and a thwarted self-understanding, perhaps even the "resentment of a defeated nation" towards the victor America.

Another cause of the critical German attitude towards the United States has stemmed from two main points since Ronald Reagan took office in November 1980. On the one hand, the Europeans and especially the Germans were alarmed by the American President's repeated references to "a limited nuclear war." On the other hand, a feeling of sheer envy arose among the Left, the Right, and "alternative melancholiacs" at the Reagan Administration's emerging economic success. The vitality of American society, the flexibility of the Americans, the absence of government red tape, the encouragement of small and medium-scale businesses, together with the American virtues of courage, initiative, mobility and willingness to adapt cannot be realized under the FRG's rigid and bureaucratic system without deep-ranging fundamental changes.

Since Helmut Kohl took office, personal relations between the Chancellor and the President seemed to have returned to normal. Until "Bitburg," they were as good as they had been between Erhard and Johnson. However, Kohl's positive view of America and Reagan has not yet had an impressive influence on German public opinion. Perhaps this is no longer possible in a "post American era."

The political, economic and military problems have multiplied since the Seventies. New priorities and interests are crystallizing in the US-European and the US-German relationships. A postulated economic and technical regression in Europe has prompted the Americans to look for new business partners in Japan and other areas of the Pacific.[57] Consensus within the Alliance seems to be crumbling:

> "Europe's endemic security question 'will in case of emergency the
> US retaliate?' (a question that General de Gaulle already answered

with an unambiguous 'no') reflects today more than ever before the crisis within the Atlantic Alliance. The problem is that the NATO-consensus is being steadily eroded, as is clear from the growing chorus of very established American voices—from Kissinger's *Brussels speech* (1979) through the Kennan-Bundy and McNamara *Foreign Affairs* articles (1982)—stressing that the halcyon days of the extended nuclear umbrella are, or should be, over. In other words, a less pronounced nuclear and more conventional emphasis on US commitment in Europe is increasingly being claimed as a matter of necessity or, even, already of fact."[58]

Despite their increasing conventional efforts, the Europeans still need the US nuclear umbrella. However, no decision has been made on European participation in the American SDI-Space-Research program. It is more uncertain than ever just how valid NATO's deterrence policy still is. Fred C. Ikle's article, "Nuclear Strategy," in *Foreign Affairs* (Spring 1985) expresses the doubtfulness of a continuing acceptance of the previously adopted military doctrine in the West.

There can be hardly any doubt about Helmut Kohl's loyalty to the Alliance. Nonetheless, the Christian-Liberal reformulation of Helmut Schmidt's *security partnership with the East* into Kohl's *joint German-German responsibility* and the related policy of close ties to the GDR caused new worry in Washington and the American press. In fact, the German question has been up in the air since Kohl took office. There are tendencies which appear to point towards the "inevitability of German unification." In August 1984, Gerd Bucrius wrote in *Die Zeit*: "I hold the reunification with the Germans in the GDR for inevitable, although remote. It would require that the citizens over there decide in a free vote on reunification. We might have to make concessions in our own social system—reunification ought to be worth it. Freedom must remain sacred, but we must be able to discuss the structure of the economy. And that can be painful." Minister of State Alois Mertes re-emphasized this in October 1984 in the *International Herald Tribune:* "Yes, West Germany Wants German Unity."

The majority of the German people do regard the problems of German reunification with a stoic calm if not actual indifference. And the majority of German politicians adhere to the provisions of the Eastern Treaties. The SPD Parliamentarian, Dietrich Stobbe, underlined in his lecture at Johns Hopkins University in October 1984: "The FRG's constitution speaks of national unity, not of reunification." Stobbe views all the talk about reunification to be "politically chic." Furthermore, Stobbe continued, the unit of a nation is not necessarily an historic given, as Yugoslav and Belgian states illustrate. After all, there is no movement for reunification with Austria. One simply had to proceed from the realities created by the Second World War, and these included the existence of two German states which are "different, but not alien."[59]

> "The new German quest for identity suddenly developing new thrust no longer places reunification in the foreground. Instead it focuses more on a kind of a 'two-state patriotism,' which hopes to create new room for more independent intra-German action as a result of establishing a more distant relationship to the respective leading powers. . . . As established detente structures were called in question the trend towards a type of German-German thinking attempting to by-pass the superpower positions was strengthened. . . . A separate German-German detente, one that attempts to ignore the fact that there is a superpower confrontation is doomed to failure. . . . The only real progress in the East-West relationship for Berlin, for Germany came—significantly enough—in the framework of a functioning cooperative relationship between the United States and the Soviet Union."[60]

President von Wizsäcker declared at the Rome meeting of the Bergedorf Discussion Group in December 1984 that he considered the extensive discussions about reunification and the open German question to be unfortunate, since "the German question had never really belonged to the Germans alone."

In the middle of a newly awoken patriotism and welling national emotions for the German past and the German question, Kohl decided to take the opportunity offered by President Reagan's Bonn visit, to combine the 40th anniversary of World War II's end with a domestic and foreign reconciliation (and to affect the elections in May). "Was reconciliation needed" asked James Markham in the *New York Times* (May 1, 1985), after the Americans 40 years ago supported the Germans economically, politically and militarily, and had become close allies and friends? If, however, a German-American reconciliation gesture was so desired by Bonn, then why did the Chancellor convince Reagan to pay a joint visit to the German soldier cemetery in Bitburg, as an inside government memorandum for his America-trip last winter had suggested? "We cannot be interested," said the memo to Kohl, "in such a one-sided view which only considers the perspective of the extermination of the Jewish people" (*Die Zeit,* April 19, 1985). The Chancellor would have better served both German democracy and his friend Ronald Reagan, especially after the President's Bitburg visit aroused such vehement opposition in the United States, image of the "ugly German" ran for three weeks in the American media, and even more so after German-American relations were threatened by the anti-Americanism of Pacifists, neutralists, Greens and Alternatives, had he allowed his Bitburg-vision to fade away.

Reconciliation has long been a reality for the new democratic Germany. And the Germans have every reason to be proud of themselves. Is that not enough? Where is the Federal Republic heading? What will be the future of NATO and the role of the Germans within the Alliance? Will the German-American relationship one day form a new German-American friendship? Elements of anti-Americanism have made themselves felt from Hegel to the Greens. The wounds of German history are still open. Only when the Germans have found their identity and are satisfied with themselves will anti-Americanism end. When, and how this will come about, no one can answer today.

NOTES

1. Quoted in *Die Zeit,* No. 46, November 9, 1984, p. 1.

2. See R.G. Livingston, "Once Again, The German Question," *German Studies Newsletter* (The Center for European Studies, Harvard University), April 1984, No. 2, p. 11-15.

3. See J. Vinocur's coverage in *The New York Times* and in that paper's Sunday Magazine from "The German Malaise," *NYT-Magazine,* Nov. 15, 1981, through "Europe's Intellectuals and American Power," *ibid.* April 29, 1984, p. 60-78.

4. See Berndt v. Staden, "Germans and Americans—Irritations," *Aussenpolitik* (engl. edition), vol. 35, January 1984.

5. President Carstens' speech is printed and published by the *Presse- und Informationsamt der Bundesreigierung,* Nr. 517, 83, Bonn 1983, p. 8.

6. President Reagan's remarks are quoted from his interview with *France Soir Magazine,* November 3, 1984: "America is 'Inextricably' linked to Europe."

7. See here Thomas Piltz (ed.), *Die Deutschen und die Amerikaner,* Munchen 1977 (p. 69 ff, List of famous German immigrants); see also Klaus

West/Heinz Moos (eds.), *300 Jahre deutsche Einwanderer in Nordamerika,* Munchen/Baltimore 1983, and Gunter Moltmann (ed.), *Germans to America. 300 Years of Immigration, 1683-1983,* Stuttgart 1982.

8. The quotation as well as parts of the arguments are taken from a lecture, "Deutschland und die Vereinigten Staaten: Historische Gleichartigkeiten und ihr Niederschlag in der Einstellung zur Aussenpolitik," by Gordon A. Craig, which he gave in Bonn at the Inter Nationes Center, November 29, 1983. Karl Kietrich Bracher held the introduction.

9. See also G.A. Craig's book, *The Germans,* New York 1982.

10. The quotations are drawn from Ernest Fraenkel, *Amerika im Spiegel des deutschen politischen Derkens,* Köln/Oplader 1959; and Alexander Ritter (ed.), *Deutschlands literarisches Amerikabild,* Hildesheim 1977; see also Manfred Henningsen, *Der Fall Amerika. Zur Sozial—und Bewusstseinsgeschichte einer Verdrangung,* Munchen 1974.

11. On Americanism during the Weimar Republic see T. Luddecke, "Amerikanismus als Schlagwort und Tatsache," *Deutsche Rundschau,* 1930, vol. 222; see also P. Berg, *Deutschland und Amerika 1918-1929, Über das deutsche Amerikabild der zwanziger Jahre,* Hamburg/Lübeck 1963 and W. Link, *Die amerikanische Stabilisierungspolitik in Deutschland, 1921-1932,* Düsseldorf 1970.

12. See G. Moltmann, "Deutscher Anti-Amerikanismus heute und früher," in F. Otmar (ed.): *Vom Sinn der Geschichte,* Stuttgart 1976, p. 85-105 and G. Wirsing: *Der masslose Kontinent,* Jena 1942.

13. The quotations are drawn from Hartmut Wasser, *Die USA—der unbekannte Partner,* Paderborn 1983, p. 29, 30.

14. For the revisionist view of the German radical Right see B.E. Schönborn, *Los von Amerika. Eine nationaldemokratische Analyse,* Kalbach 1974; C.B. Dalls, *Amerikas Driegspolitik, Roosevelt und seine Hintermänner,* Tübingen 1975; B. Colby, *Roosevelts scheinheiliger Krieg,* Berg, 1977; H. Fish, *Der zerbrochene Mythos. F.D. Roosevelts Kriegspolitik 1933-1945,* Berg 1982; J. Bruhn/D. Bauendamm, *Roosevelts Weg zum Krieg,* München 1983. For the revisionist view of the German marxist Left see A. Charisius et. al., *Weltgendarm USA,* Berlin 1983; G. Kade, *Die Amerikaner und wir,* Köln 1983; B. Grüner/K. Steinhaus, *Auf dem Weg zum 3. Weltkrieg? Amerikanische Kriegspläne gegen die UdSSR, Eine Dokumentation,* Köln 1980.

15. See H. Wasser, *Das deutsche Amerika-bild nach 1945—Spiegel oder Zerrbild?* op. cit., p. 32, and Günther C. Behrmann, "Geschichte und aktuelle Struktur des Antiamerikanismus," *Aus Politik und Zeitgeschichte,* B 29-30/1984, p. 3-14. See also James F. Tent, *Mission on the Rhine: Reeducation and Denazification in American-occupied Germany,* Chicago 1983, University of Chicago Press. See Avi Shlaim, *The United States and the Berlin Blockade, 1948-49: A Study in Crisis Decision Making,* Berkeley 1983, University of California Press.

16. The quotation is taken from Konrad Adenauer's memoirs: *Erinnerungen,* vol. 1: 1945-1953, Stuttgart 1968. On German-American relations after World War II, see Ernst-Otto Czempiel, *"Die Bundesrepublik und Amerika: Von der Okkupation zur Kooperation,"* in *Die Zweite Republik, 25 Jahre Bundesrepublik Deutschland—Eine Bilanz,* (Ed.), R. Lowenthal/H.P. Schwarz, Stuttgart 1974/79; (Ed.,) Manfred Knapp, *Die deutsch-amerikanischen Beziehungen nach 1945,* Frankfurt/M. 1975; Roger Morgan, *Washington und Bonn, Deutsch-amerikanische Beziehungen seit dem Zweiten Weltkrieg,* München 1975; Uwe Nehrlich, "Washington und Bonn: Entwicklungsstrukturen im deutsch-amerikanischen Verhältnis," in *Amerika und Westeuropa,* (ed. K. Kaiser/H.-P. Schwarz), Stuttgart/Zurich 1977.

17. Wrote Richard E. Neustadt: "In the Adenauer era, and thereafter for a time, it scarcely seemed to matter whether we guessed right or wrong about what moved a German player in his own game or how our own moves resonated inside his own machine. . . We then possessed a wide latitude for ignorance," *Alliance Politics,* New York and London: Columbia Univ. Press, 1970, p. 143.

18. See Karl W. Deutsch, "Amerikanische Deutschlandpolitik," *Politik und Kultur,* vol. 11, No. 1, 1984, p. 3-15, and Peter Bender's critical essay: "Amerikanische Deutschlandpolitik: Ein realistisches Wiedervereinigungskonzept hat es nie gegeben," *Deutschland Archiv,* August 1984 (8), p. 830-833.

19. See G.C. Behrmann, op. cit., and also Wolfgang Wagner, "Das Amerikabild der Europäer," in *Amerika and Westeuropa,* op. cit., p. 17-28.

20. See Waldemar Besson, *Die Aussenpolitik der Bundesrepublik,* Müchen 1972; Walter Stützle, *Kennedy und Adenauer in der Berlin-Krise 1961-1962,* Bonn-Bad Godesberg 1973; R. Morgan, op. cit., p. 101.

21. See here Karl Dietrich Bracher, *Das deutsche Dilemma, Leidenswege der politischen Emanzipation,* Munchen 1971, and also Hans-Joachim Arndt, *Die Besiegten von 1945, Versuch einer Politologie fur Deutsche, samt Wurdigung der Politikwissenschaft in der Bundesrepublik Deutschland,* 1978.

22. See Chapter 8, "America: Custodian of the world" of Vaughn Davis Bornet's book, *The Presidency of Lyndon B. Johnson,* University of Kansas, 1983, p. 169.

23. Quotation is taken from: R. Morgan, op. cit., p. 141 f.

24. See Georg von Lilienfeld, "Besuch bei John F. Kennedy (1963)", in *Begegnungen mit Kurt Georg Kiesinger (Festgabe zum 80. Geburtstag),* (ed.) Dieter Oberndorfer, Stuttgart 1984.

25. Quoted from US-Embassy Bonn-Telegrams to Department of State, Oct. 10, 1966: Subj.: Impact of Erhard Visit; Oct. 14, 1966: Subj.: Conversation with Jean Monnet (Harriman/Archives)

26. Quoted from US-Embassy Bonn-Telegram to Department of State, Oct. 14, 1966: Subj.: Attitude of German Industry Leaders towards Erhard (Harriman/Archives).

27. Walt W. Rostow, *View From the Seventh Floor,* New York 1964, p. 70 f.

28. Quoted from Marion Gräfin Dönhoff, *Amerikanische Wechselbäder,* Stuttgart 1983, p. 119.

29. Quoted from the *Memorandum of Conversation* between Secretary Rusk, Under Secretary Ball and Chancellor Erhard, Foreign Minister Schröder at Blair House, Sept. 25, 1966 (Harriman/Archives).

30. Quoted from *The Memorandum For The President And The Secretary Of State,* Oct. 3, 1966, by W. Averell Harriman, Subj.: Negotiations (Harriman/Archives).

31. See H.G. Lehmann, *Öffnung nach Osten,* Bonn-Bad Godesberg 1984 and William E. Griffith, ''The German Problem and American Policy,'' *Survey,* No. 61, October 1966.

32. Both remarks were made by US-Ambassador McGhee, the first is taken from his letter to Secretary of State Rusk, American Embassy, Bonn, Germany, July 21, 1964: Subj.: Discussion with Attorney General (Robert F. Kennedy stopped in Bonn on the way from Warsaw back to Washington) on Oder-Neisse Territory; the second is taken from a US-Embassy Bonn-Telegram to Department of State, Oct. 17, 1966: Subj.: Oder-Neisse Line (Harriman/Archives)

33. Quoted from Department of State-Telegram to the US-Embassy in Bonn, Oct. 7, 1966; Subj.: Erhard Visit to Washington, Sept. 26-27 (Harriman/Archives).

34. Quoted from: A Transcript of a Recorded Interview with W. Averell Harriman, Interviewer: Philip A. Crowl, Washington, D.C., July 16, 1966, *The John Foster Dulles Oral History Project,* The Princeton University Library (Harriman/Archives), p. 28-33.

35. See Klaus Hildebrand, *Von Erhard zur Grossen Koalition (1963-1969),* vol. 4 from the series: ''Geschichte der Bundesrepublik Deutschland,'' op.cit., forthcoming, 1985.

36. Chancellor Kiesinger's remarks are quoted from US-Embassy Bonn-Telegram to Department of State, Dec. 21, 1966: Subj.: First meeting between Chancellor Kiesinger and Ambassador McGhee (Harriman/Archives).

37. See R. Morgan, op. cit., p. 155 ff.

38. See H.G. Lehmann, op. cit.

39. See Theo Sommer, ''Bonn's New Ostpolitik,'' *Journal of International Affairs,* vol. 22, 1968, No. 1.

40. See Waldemar Besson, "The Conflict of Traditions," in, *Britain and West Germany*, (eds.) K. Kaiser/R. Morgan, London: Oxford Univ. Press, 1971, p. 80.

41. Theo Sommer, "Bonn Changes Course," *Foreign Affairs*, vol. 45, 1967, p. 482-83.

42. Thesis of Professor Lily Gardner Feldman at the *Fifth New England Workshop On German Affairs*, "Perception and Misperception in International Relations: the Federal Republic of Germany and the United States, 1960-1983," Tufts University, May 10-12, 1984.

43. See Willy Brandt's memoirs, *Begegnungen und Einsichten, Die Jahre 1960-1975* (Chapter 3: John F. Kennedy), Hamburg 1976; David Binder, *The Other German. Willy Brandt's Life and Times,* Washington, D.C. 1976.

44. See Richard Löwenthal, *Vom Kalten Drieg zur Ostpolitik,* Stuttgart 1974; Arnulf Baring (in cooperation with Manfred Görtemaker): *Machtwechsel, Die Ära Brandt-Scheel,* Stuttgart 1982; Gerard Braunthal, *The West German Social Democrats, 1969-1982: Profile of a Party in Power,* Boulder/Colorado, 1983.

45 See U. Nehrlich, op. cit., p. 340 f.

46. See John Lewis Gaddis, *Strategies of Containment, A Critical Appraisal of Postwar American National Security Policy,* Oxford: Oxford Univ. Press, 1982; M. Mathiopoulos, "Zur Containment-Politik der USA: Strategien von Roosevelt bis Reagan," *Politik und Kultur,* No. 3, 1983.

47. Henry Kissinger, *White House Years (1969-1973),* Boston/Toronto 1979, p. 424.

48. H. Kissinger, op. cit., p. 409, p. 529.

49. Interview with West Germany's Chancellor Willy Brandt "What Europe wants from US," *U.S. News and World Report,* April 30, 1973.

50. See Zbigniew Brzezinski, "The European Crossroads," in *Atlantis Lost, U.S.-European Relations after the Cold War,* (eds. James Chace/Earl C. Ravenal) New York Univ. Press 1976; Stanley Hoffman, *Primacy or World Order, American Foreign Policy since the Cold War,* New York et. al. 1980; Helmut Schmidt, "The Struggle for the World Product, Politics between Power and Morals," *Foreign Affairs,* April 1974.

51. See K.W. Deutsch, op. cit. See also Herbert Woopen, "Dürfen die europäischen NATO-Staaten ihre Streitkräfte ausserhalb des NATO-Gebiets einsetzen?," *Neue Zeitschrift fur Wehrrecht,* 1983, p. 201 ff.

52. Jimmy Carter: *Keeping Faith, Memoirs of A President,* Toronto/New York/London/Sydney 1982, p. 113.

53. Z. Brzezinski, *Power and Principle, Memoirs of the National Security Advisor 1977-1981,* New York, 1983, p. 26, p. 291.

54. J. Carter, op. cit., p. 538.

55. See Kim F. Holmes, *The West Germany peace Movement and the National Question,* Cambridge, Mass.: Institute for Foreign Policy Analysis, 1984; Robert L. Pfaltzgraff et al., *The Greens of West Germany: Origins, Strategies, and Trans-atlantic Implictions,* Cambridge, Mass.: Institute for Foreign Policy Analysis, 1983; Kendall L. Baker/Russell J. Dalton/Kai Hildebrandt, *Germany Transformed: Political Culture and The New Politics,* Cambridge, Mass./London: Harvard Univ. Press, 1981; H.P. Wallach/G.K. Romoser, *West German Politics in the Mid-Eighties, Crisis and Continuity,* New York, February 1985; Jeffrey Herf, "Unpublished manuscript on German nationalism and the peace movement," Harvard Univ. 1984. On the American view of Germany see Heinz Schneppen, "Zum Deutschenbild in den Vereinigten Staaten," *Europa-Archiv,* No. 18, 1983. On American press- and media-reports on Germany, see Anita M. Mallinckrodt, "Medienberichterstatung über die Bundesrepublik in den USA," *Aus Politik und Zeitgeschichte,* B 29-30/84, p. 15 ff.

56. Richard von Weizsäcker, *Die deutsche Geschichte geht weiter,* Berlin 1983, p. 299. See Theodor Eschenburg, *Jahre der Besatzung 1945-1949,* vol. 1 from the series "Geschichte der Bundesrepublik Deutschland," op. cit., 1983; Bundesarchiv/Institut fur Zeitgeschichte (ed.), *Akten zur Vorgeschichte der Bundesrepublk Deutschland 1945 bis 1949,* 5 vols., München 1976-1983, and the documentation by Hans-Jörg Ruhl, *Neubeginn und Restauration, Dokumente zur Vorgeschichte der Bundesrepublik Deutschland 1945-1949,* Müchen 1982; Rolf Steiniger, *Deutsche Geschichte 1945-1961—Darstellung und Dokumente in zwei Bänden,* Frankfurt/M. 1983; Wilfried Loth, "Träume vom Deutschen Reich," *Die Zeit,* Oct. 12, 1984, p. 73.

57. See Jan Reifenberg, "Atlantische irritationen, Werden die Vereinigten Staaten und Europa weiter auseinanderrücken?", *Frankfurter Allgemeine Zeitung,* September 1, 1984.

58. Jacobus Delwaide, *TNF-Issue and European Insecurity,* unpublished manuscript, Harvard Univ. 1982; see also Manfred Görtemaker, "Bündnis mit Zukunft, Krisen and Strukturveranderungen erfordern eine Umgrundung der Atlantischen Allianz," *Der Monat* (special issue: Europa und Amerika, Ende einer Ära), No. 20, February 1984.

59. Informal talk with Dietrich Stobbe MdB, November 30, 1984 in Bonn. On German-German relations from the point of view of the GDR see the article by Günter Gaus in the *German Studies Newsletter,* Nov. 1984, No. 3.

60. D. Stobbe, speech at the "American Institute for Contemporary German Studies," Johns Hopkins University, unpublished manuscript.

CHAPTER 4

THE U.S. PRESIDENCY: AN AUSTRIAN PERSPECTIVE

Oliver Rathkolb

The Austrian perspective of the American presidency is the "squaring of the circle between western parliamentarianism and American presidentialism."[1] A strong political heritage of parliamentary government has left its impact on the Austrian view of the United States. Austria has had a form of parliamentary government since the constitution of 1920. Its view of the American presidency is also shaped by its own national sentiments toward the executive branch. The highest executive office is divided in Austria. The federal government is represented by the Federal Chancellor, who has by far the most politically relevant executive functions. The head of state is the Federal President, who is elected by the Federal Assembly (that is, both "houses" of Parliament, the National and Federal Councils).

This "deprivation of power" of the executive is based on the fact that, after the end of the monarchy in 1918, the designers of the Constitution wanted to avoid the possible absolutism of the head of state at all costs. The result was that the provisional constitution initially made no provision for a head of state at all. The functions of the head of state were to be discharged by the President of the National Assembly.[2] A Federal President was not elected until 1920. In 1929, when the Constitution was partially revised, there was an attempt to remodel the office of the Federal President on the Weimar Republic by strengthening it through national elections and an extension of powers. However, the feared presidential dictatorship never came about because Parliament was dissolved in 1933 and Austria was "annexed" by Germany in 1938. It was not until after 1945 that the socio-economic infrastructure was created to guarantee the decidedly parliamentary form of government.

In addition to the parliamentary slant, the Austrian perspective has been influenced by individual American presidents. Early impressions were formed during the AustroHungarian Monarchy, the First Republic of 1918-1933, and the periods of Austro-Fascism from 1933-1938 and National Socialism from 1938-1945. The image of the US was further shaped during the Allied occupation of Austria from 1945-1955. The US presidents after the Second World War made their own impact on Austria. These impressions of individual presidents have contributed considerably to the general picture of America.

Perceptions of the American presidency are shaped by institutions as well as individuals. The electoral process of US presidents is baffling to Austrians. The political power and decision-making of the president are also misunderstood. Finally, the personalisation of the presidency, particularly by the media, has also distorted the Austrian perspective.

This analysis of the American presidency will first consider the impact of individual presidents. Some of the most influential presidents in shaping the European viewpoint were Woodrow Wilson, Franklin D. Roosevelt, the post-World War II presidents, and recent presidents. Then the analysis turns to the institution of the American presidency and the influence of the media. Particularly since the end of the Second World War, those interested in foreign political events have received much information on the US via the media. This conglomerate of stereotyped ideas about the US can only be disentangled with difficulty.

Dominant Presidential Images in the 20th Century

Thomas Woodrow Wilson

There were no direct presidential relations with the Hapsburg Monarchy. Although both George Washington and Abraham Lincoln are found in Austrian history books, they appear as idealized incarnations of pure democracy and of the abolition of slavery. For the Central European empire, America appeared as the mythical land of unlimited economic and social opportunity, which attracted millions of immigrants like a magnet. In addition, the "Wild West" flavor provided excitement in literature and the press. This idealization of the US and of American presidents was shattered by the disappointment over Woodrow Wilson.

The presidential image of the first half of the 20th century was influenced by Wilson's "Fourteen Points" of 8 January 1918. On the one hand, the Fourteen Points supported the national feelings of various peoples of the Monarchy, and, on the other, called up false hopes of a postwar order in Europe based wholly on ethnic criteria. The German-speaking "Austrian remnant" was all the more disappointed after the Treaty of St. Germain of 1919 when it was not permitted by the Entente to enter into a union with the Germany of the Weimar Republic. The name Deutsch-Usterreich (German-Austria), which had been proclaimed in 1918, could no longer be used. South Tyrol, which was almost totally German-speaking, was finally lost to Italy, as were the German-speaking pockets on the southern borders of Czechoslovakia.

President Wilson's inability to insist on the right to self-determination for the "German-Austrians," against the wishes of his European allies, and the fact that the American Congress voted against joining the League of Nations greatly influenced the image of the American president in the subsequent decades. Wilson was seen as a great moralist who was, however, unable to prevail in the traditional trial of strength between the great powers. He was considered to be weak. Both the political decision-makers and the general public of Austria clearly overestimated the power of the presidency and saw the country as an imperial presidential republic. This was understandable since the Austrians themselves had had only very limited experience with democracy in the AustroHungarian Monarchy after 1948.

This disappointment over Wilson could not be compensated for by American aid and the food for children program. However, these programs at least laid a foundation for the ideological success of the Marshall Plan. America was thought of as a generous nation ready to help, an impression that was strengthened under President Hoover.

Franklin Delano Roosevelt

For a long time Austrian public life was dominated by its own substantial economic and social problems. These problems resulted in the authoritarian dictatorship of Austro-Fascism in 1933, a civil war between the Social Democrats and Communists, a Nazi putsch, and the murder of the dictator Dollfuss by the Austrian National Socialists in 1934. The ruling elite of the Clerical Fascists in Austria viewed Franklin D. Roosevelt's New Deal with great scepticism.

The image of Roosevelt in the "German Empire," which swallowed up Austria after the "Anschluss" of 1938, was formed by the National Socialist propaganda. He was seen as a weak president (analogous to a "decadent democracy"), despite the considerable power that he embodied. After the US entered the war in 1941 he was classified as a mediocre politician who was only distinguished by great vitality and the effects of widespread propaganda.

This basic tenor continued after Roosevelt's death—especially with regard to the Allied postwar plans in which he was very open to the Soviet expansionist desire to create a broad buffer zone around the Soviet Union in Eastern Europe. His efforts to establish world order for peace, which finally brought about the creation of the United Nations, are often forgotten. Moreover, academic discussion of Roosevelt's role in the nascent East-West conflict put forth the theory that the gap between rhetoric and policy is not only a central problem in judging the strength of Roosevelt's personality, but a problem of American democratic foreign policy per se that is hard to resolve. At any rate, Roosevelt's foreign policy is often reduced to the effects of the Yalta Conference.

From Truman to Eisenhower to Kennedy

The Viennese National Socialist press reported the nomination of the US Senator Harry Truman as the Democratic Party's candidate for Vice-President at the end of 1944 in unusual detail. This was clearly set against a background of Roosevelt's poor state of health. Truman's simple origins, his image as an honest American citizen, and the machinations of the Pendergast election machine were all stressed. His membership in the right wing of the party was emphasized—perhaps to fuel the unjustified hope that US foreign policy towards Germany might change course on the death of Roosevelt.

This polemical image of Truman during the Nazi period was confronted with official American foreign propaganda in mid-1945. Through their own radio station "Rot-Weiss-Rot," newspaper "Wiener Kurier," press agency, and exchange programs, the American Occupation Forces in Austria exercised a direct influence on the image of the President from 1945 to 1955.[3] The intentions of the original re-education program were to idealize the advantages of the American democratic system and present them uncritically.

This colorless reporting on America—apart from the verbal polemics of the Communist press which had only a small circulation—continued into the Eisenhower presidency. In particular, reports on the President lacked the opportunity to identify with Austrian concerns, since the 40s and 50s were dominated by strong Secretaries of State like Marshall, Acheson, and Dulles, who were household names to the people. In sum, positive reporting on America predominated—especially because of the European Recovery Program which seemed to perpetuate the ideological and economic integration of Austria into the Western camp.

The deepest impression of all US presidents was that of John F. Kennedy. His way of presenting his policies was the nonplus ultra for a whole generation in Austria. His inaugural speech was printed on the front page of almost all newspapers. For the first time ever, not only the foreign policy section of his ambitious program was noted, but also those policies concerned with internal American problems, like racial integration. The Kennedy myth, which coincided with the start of economic prosperity in Austria, was not restricted to public opinion, but also had an effect on the political decision-makers. For example, the long-term Austrian Foreign Minister (1959-1966) and later Federal Chancellor (1970-1982) Bruno Kreisky, thought Kennedy was a "fascinating personality with very similar political ideas."[4] The reports of Kennedy's assassination were a great shock to Austria since he was—not least through the Vienna summit meeting with Khruschev in 1961—extraordinarily popular in Austria.

Johnson, Nixon, Ford, Carter and Reagan

Just as the positive image of Kennedy was exaggerated in Austria, that of his successor was equally slanted. No longer was there a committed liberal young father with a beautiful wife, but instead a calculating rancher and grandfather from Texas. Thus, it is not surprising that no one actually links the name of Lyndon Johnson with the great social programs of his presidency, but only with the escalation of the Viet Nam War, even though the roots of that conflict lay in the Kennedy era. This paradox can be partly explained by the fact that, in the mid-60s, both in the Federal Republic of Germany and in Austria, the process of emancipation began, especially in the younger generation. This emancipation started to dismantle the uncritical and uncomplicated view of America that had been promoted since 1945. The US, and thereby the office of the President were increasingly less often presented as the absolute ideal of a pluralistic democracy and materially affluent society. This new Marxist picture of America was, however, just as fuzzy as the euphorically naive democratic one. Only thus can the demonstration in Salzburg, on the occasion of a short visit by President Richard Nixon in 1972, be explained. With the increasing escalation of the Viet Nam War, the role and importance of the American President was increasingly reduced to this single item of foreign policy.

However, Watergate also had a great effect on political consciousness in Europe, not least because until then the fiction had been maintained that the American President had to be a man of lonely decisions. Particularly since Kennedy, the success or failure of political measures had been wholly ascribed to the President alone. It is noteworthy that despite all criticism of Nixon's behavior in the Watergate affair, his achievements for detente have remained uncontested. Thus, for example, Kreisky was always convinced that Nixon would end the Viet Nam War.[5] A high-ranking Austrian diplomat, Hans J. Thalberg, even put forth in his memoirs the theory that the sharply anti-Soviet attitude of Richard Nixon and his rapprochement with China were necessary to create a milder climate between the two superpowers and to dissuade Moscow from further adventures.[6] He generalized his statement by offering the paradox that severely anti-Soviet governments in Washington are better able to deal with Moscow than the liberal politicans who are much closer to the Europeans.

In the light of this thesis which frequently reduces the complicated political and economic interaction between the two great powers to much too simple a formula, the policies of Ford and Carter are defined as too reticent. The Iranian hostage crisis had an especially important effect on public opinion in this respect. The view of American political economists that the rise of Jimmy Carter produced a Bonapartite feudal system[17]—as a consequence of the "imperial presidency" under Nixon—has never found any echo in Austria. Carter's missionary and charismatic rhetoric was seen rather, from the viewpoint of "realpolitik", as a weakness.

Nevertheless, the verbally strong policies of Ronald Reagan have only met with limited approval. Austrians have been primarily and surprisingly interested in his foreign policy despite the fact that the above-average strength of the dollar is a brake on Austrian export trade and keeps energy costs high despite large market surpluses. Part of this interest in Reagan's foreign policy is from the opposition party, the Austrian People's Party (OUP), which is only interested in foreign policy questions like American policy towards Nicaragua. On the other side, Kreisky speaks openly of the unpredictability of Reagan which, in his opinion, has brought a new and dangerous component into US foreign policy.[8] In addition, the media reporting is more concerned with Reagan's advisors than under previous Presidents because the White House, rather than the State Department, dominates. This effect is strengthened by the phenomenon that Austrians are used to seeing academics or career politicians with long experience as party political functionaries at the head of various centers of power. Thus, they are nonplused by the fact that a former film actor—whose films have been rebroadcast in recent years by the sole Austrian TV station—is now head of the US. His period as Governor of California is usually only mentioned in relation to his closest advisors, most recently in the reshuffle of January 1985.

The Austrian perception of the American presidency has made dramatic shifts in the twentieth century. The idealized myths of George Washington and Abraham Lincoln dissipated when Woodrow Wilson's promises of self-determination were not realized. This darkly tinted perception of the American president continued with Franklin D. Roosevelt and the effects of the Yalta Conference. It was Harry Truman and the political climate after the Second World War that brought about a shift in perception. America and the presidency were again idealized, this time through the media which focused on positive reporting. John F. Kennedy was the pinnacle in this upward shift. With the escalation of the Viet Nam War, the American presidency again suffered a loss of esteem which was compounded by the perception of Jimmy Carter as weak and the limited approval of Ronald Reagan.

Austrian Perceptions of the US Presidency

The Electoral Process

The most significant difference between the American and Austrian concepts of a democratic presidency—apart from the extent of the sphere of competence of the US President—lies in the method of selection. Today the Austrian Federal President is elected directly by the Austrian people for a period of six years. This constitutional measure was first realised in 1951. Previously, all Austrian Federal Presidents had been elected by the Federal Assembly. This assembly consists of the politically relevant National Council and the almost exclusively symbolic Federal Council. The Federal Council is intended to provide the federal component with at least a hearing.

The concept of an indirect election of the Federal President was also contained in the original version of the first democratic Constitution of the Republic of Austria of 1920, two years after the break-up of the Hapsburg Empire. The Social Democrats, however, favored the American pattern. The Social Democrat State Chancellor, Karl Renner, referred to the exemplary "institution of primary elections within the parties during the presidential elections in the United States."[9] The Social Democrats feared that a direct election would enable the power of the President to become too great through its direct legitimacy, and be misused to form a dictatorship by popular tribune. Despite all their misgivings, they did, however, agree to the change in the Constitution of 1929. However, this was never put into practice, since the Constitution was broken in 1933 and replaced by the Austro-Fascist "Estates Constitution." Finally, in 1938 Hitler put a violent end to any possible elections. It is noteworthy that, despite the severe criticism in 1929 of the change in the Constitution, this solution was kept in 1945. In 1929, legal experts and politicans feared that strengthening the position of the Federal President could lead to Austria being maneuvered into the ranks of the fascist-bolshevist states. It was not until after 1945 that the socio-economic climate was sufficiently stabilized for national elections not to be deemed authoritarian.

In contrast, Austrians today have great difficulty understanding the indirect system of the US presidential elections through an electoral college. They tend to consider this system antiquated, although the Austrian tradition of direct elections is by no means old. In addition, Austrians have problems understanding the elections. For example, the provision that all the electoral college votes are given to the candidate who won a simple majority in that state is seen as undemocratic.

Even more astonishment is produced by another fact: there is no duty to vote, but the voters must register to vote before—as with other elections for the Senate or the House of Representatives—they have any right to vote at all. The relatively low electoral participation is equally incomprehensible. Although Austrian traditions are not very old—the general franchise for men has existed only since 1906 and for women since 1918—Austria does put modern electoral criteria of a technical nature into practice.

Moreover, in television reports and the Nixon memoirs, mention is repeatedly made of electoral manipulation through adjustment of the voting machine. The voting machine is viewed with deep scepticism in Austria. Voting in Austria is still by paper ballot. This, however, is not 100 percent foolproof against manipulation, despite observers from the most important parties. Particularly in totalitarian regimes this method is of no use at all, as illustrated in Austrian history. There was an almost 100 percent plebiscite in favour of the "Anschluss" with Hitler's

Germany after 1938, whereas the previous poll under the Schuschnigg regime produced a 60-70 percent pro-Austrian majority.

The Austrian State Chancellor of the First and Second Republics and Federal President Renner supported the system of primary elections as the ideal form of public democratic choice without pressure of time. In contrast, the Austrian Foreign Minister (1945-1953) and Ambassador to Washington in 1954-1958 and 1969-1972, Karl Gruber, considered the quota system in the party committees of the Democratic Party to be dangerous. Gruber's opinion can be illustrated by the electoral campaign of Senator McGovern: it can lead to the entrenched functionaries being unable to prevail over peripheral forces.[10] In principle, the author is of the opinion that a basic democracy, as such, is to be welcomed but that it contradicts the Austrian system of functionary politics. However, even in the Austrian system, changes are beginning to appear, particularly with respect to the environmental movement which is scratching at the old, fossilized party structures.

Most Austrians have a false impression of the American party system and its influence on the President. The European political parties are strictly organized at the regional and supraregional levels. Whatever the internal sectional struggles may be, they profess loyalty to the same party program. Party discipline keeps the rank and file together, while the party whip in Parliament ensures the requisite votes for the party line. By European criteria, the American parties are anti-parties in the sense of an old quip from the 20s: "I'm not a member of any organized political party, I'm a Democrat."[11] This strict and narrow understanding of the party also explains the belief that the American President cannot always successfully oppose his party. This is considered a weakness from the point of view of the narrow European party tradition.

The mass media seizes on the primaries and reports extensively on the spectacle. During the last presidential elections Austrian television covered the American electoral night nonstop until far into the morning. The excessive US presidential primaries are considerably more wearing and expensive than Austrian voting campaigns. In recent years, however, the American influence has been increasingly noticeable here. Nonetheless, for the average Austrian, this style of electoral campaign primarily represents a successful circus or show. With respect to its effect on the image of the office of the President as such, it should be mentioned that each US President is credited with a strong element of showmanship in his activities. Concrete details, however, do not remain in the consciousness. Even the inaugural addresses of the Presidents are forgotten, despite extensive media coverage, with the exception of Kennedy.

Political Power

Whereas the Austrian Federal President exercises primarily representative functions and has, in practice, no real political power, the American system of presidential democracy is seized with a considerably larger sphere of competence. However, this difference is precisely what often causes the overestimation of the absolute power of the US President in real political terms. While some of those responsible for making decisions in Austria are aware of the role of Congress, the American system is quite foreign to the average Austrian. This is strengthened by the fact that the Austrian Federal Chancellor, who is roughly equivalent to the US President in his sphere of competence, is not subject to political influence so long as his own party or coalition in Parliament possesses an absolute majority. The party boundaries are much more fixed in Austria than in the US system. It was incomprehensible to the Austrians that Nixon who was able to hold out for so long, resigned when it was certain that he would otherwise be impeached. This reinforced the exaggerated myth of the man of lonely decisions and his absolute power.

The influence of pressure groups and lobbies is, to a great extent, unknown to the Austrian. Should an awareness of them arise here, it would be restricted to the unions and perhaps employers' representatives analogous to the Austrian system, although the latter do not exist in the US in any equivalent form. If anything, the Jewish Lobby is known, though this is unfortunately counterproductive since during the Nazi era the term was frequently misused in antisemitic propaganda.

A further restriction on the political power of the President, which is almost completely unknown, is the hearings and confirmation process in the Senate of the ministers, high officials, and diplomats appointed by the President. In comparison, the Austrian Federal Government is chosen by the Federal Chancellor and sworn in by the Federal President, the necessary majority in the National Council having been considered when forming the Government. Officials and diplomats are nominated by the appropriate Federal Ministers and require no democratic confirmation. This can result in individual spectacular hearings causing a sensation in the Austrian press. The journalists make fun of the lack of expert knowledge among the members of the American government, forgetting that, unfortunately, this form of democratic control does not exist in Austria. It is often presumed that this measure of publicity is a weakness for democracy. The author, however, would point out that this publicity is the most basic form of democratic control and legitimation.

The phenomenon that the office of the President is so inadequately delineated in public opinion can be sought in the fact that the sphere of competence and possibilities of the American President in domestic and socio-economic politics can hardly be realized. This function is only recognized in expert circles. Thus, for example, Roosevelt's "New Deal" and Truman's "Fair Deal" were seen by the Socialist Vice-Chancellor Scharf, (who was also Federal President from 1957 to 1965) as an example of the modern economic and investment policy that was to be a pattern for Austria in the 50s.[12] On the other hand, Johnson's social programs are still largely unknown. The best known question of domestic policy—especially under Kennedy—was that of the racial problem.

The French philosopher and statesman Alexis de Tocqueville, who visited the US at the beginning of the Jackson era, reports a very poor opinion of the presidency and its potentialities. The non-participation of the United States in external affairs in particular, is thought of poorly: "All his important acts are directly or indirectly submitted to the legislature; and where he is independent of it he can do but little."[13]

In 1908 the Ambassador of the Austro-Hungarian Monarchy reported that, during normal times, the American people had little interest in foreign affairs. "It is significant in this respect" he concluded, "that neither in the introduction to the platform . . . nor in the eulogy which Senator Lodge gave [President Roosevelt] at the opening of the Convention [of the Republican party in 1908] was there any mention of the President's accomplishments and successes in the area of foreign policy."[14] Today the interested Austrian is offered a completely different picture. In the course of the 20th century, and especially since the Second World War and the period of the Cold War, reports on America are dominated by foreign politics. The more intensively and comprehensively the US engages itself in world politics, the more the image of America in Europe is reduced to these events. Foreign reporting is increasingly becoming 'bush fire reporting' and concerns itself solely with the current centers of conflict in the world. A continuous, 'inside' coverage hardly ever appears in the newspapers any more and is relegated to minority programs on television.

As a result, Austrian knowledge of the American party system and domestic politics is extremely scanty. Where it does exist it remains primarily on an idealistic level. The socio-economic tasks and problems of the President are only mentioned as points of his program during TV or newspaper reports. Of the foreign reports in printed media, 25 percent of all contributions concern the Federal Republic of Germany and the US (the share of foreign reporting being 41.6 percent of all newspaper coverage). They are followed by Italy (5.1 percent), Great Britain (4.7 percent), France (3.9 percent) and the USSR (2.9 percent).[15] Similarly, the FRG and the US receive by far the most attention in the foreign sections of the television news.

Decision-Making

Vinzenz Ludwig Ostry was the press officer of the former Austrian Federal President and Vice-Chancellor, Adolf Scharf, and he was director of political programs for the American German-language radio station in Austria "Rot-Weiss-Rot" from 1950-1955. Prior to the 1968 presidential election, Ostry published a book about the US President entitled "The Most Powerful Man on Earth."[16] In this book he revived the fiction of the President as a man of lonely decisions. The complicated internal process of decision-making within the White House and the channels of communication to the individual members of the Government were mentioned, but their true significance was not recognized. A similar understanding of the decision-making process must also be assumed to lie in the general consciousness, despite the detailed exposés in Kissinger's memoirs and the appropriate American literature.

Whenever a decision-making process is examined, it is that of foreign policy which strengthens the overemphasis on that sector. In Germany in particular, monographs are continually being written on case studies in foreign politics, above all on the Viet Nam War. Well-researched studies of domestic politics are rather rare.

In view of the fact that, as chief executive, the President is the chief intermediary through whom all foreign relations are conducted, it must be remarked that, especially under Eisenhower, it was fully recognised that foreign policy was primarily made by Secretary of State John Foster Dulles. This has undergone a fundamental change since Kennedy. Even a strong personality like Kissinger could no longer wipe out the presidential monopoly on foreign policy, though he was able to divide it temporarily.

The bureaucratic apparatus of the White House appears completely incomprehensible and opaque, especially in the conflicts with the various ministries. Under Eisenhower, the decision-making process in foreign policy was relatively transparent with regard to administration and competences. The subsequent administrations, in contrast, have presented considerably more complicated channels of communication, which were centralized in particular by Henry Kissinger under Nixon. To avoid this confusion, a basic formula was developed whereby only the President makes the decision. Who prepares this decision, based on which options and reflecting which constellation of interests, usually remains unanswered.

A basic theme in the judgement of presidential decisions on foreign policy since the Wilson Presidency is the thesis that the Americans and their decision-makers have not experienced as much as the Europeans in the 20th century, with their two world wars. As a result, an incomprehensibly carefree attitude determines American politics. This is considered to be illusory and is distinguished by an optimism that, in the last resort, leads to disappointment. This stereotypical notion is not only deeply seated in the general opinion but also in professional foreign politicians such as, to take a concrete case, Lujo Toncic, Austrian Foreign Minister, 1966-1968.[17] One reason for this undoubtedly too simple explanation for US foreign policy in the 20th century lies in the fact that Wilson was not able to realize his proclaimed right to national self-determination in the case of "German-Austria" in 1918/1919. Another reason lies in the experience of the postwar division of Europe into spheres of influence. Roosevelt was accused, above all in the media but also in numerous publications, of having been too conciliatory to Stalin. In both cases, however, the constellation of concrete American interests at the time of these foreign policy decisions is completely left out of account, if not deliberately rejected or suppressed.

The Personalization of the Presidency

One reason for oversimplification and for a false concept of the mechanism of arriving at American foreign policy through the President is partly based on the American programs of information in Austria after 1945. Countless brochures, newspaper articles, and school books presented an exaggerated picture of the American President. Even comics, with an idealized presentation of the lives of Washington and Lincoln were distributed in large numbers. This overpositive presentation found its way once more into school books and so into the general consciousness of the population.

A further step towards the extreme privatization of political processes came through the widespread presentation of the private life of the President. His wife and children were considerably more attractive for the media. Thus, they had a more wide-reaching effect, while at the same time almost completely swamping genuine political information. The rainbow press has not been alone in indulging in this new form of "Court Circular" since Kennedy, (though its beginnings go back to Truman and Eisenhower) which totally ignores the underlying political, economic and social situation. This overprivatization of a political office often gives the foreign observer the impression that, despite all his range of power, this individual person can be easily influenced.

The media, in particular, ascribe a role here which they in sum cannot fill. The argument is very frequently put forward that in connection with the Viet Nam War coverage "in the 1960s the network organizations became 'a highly creditable, never-tiring political opposition, a maverick third party which never need face the sobering experience of governing.' "[18] This argument is strengthened by the inappropriate personalization and individualization of the duties of the US President. However, it does not stand up to research, since also in the case of Viet Nam "the media tend to be supporting or critical of government policies depending on the degree of consensus those policies enjoy, particularly within the political establishment."[19]

This overestimation of the influence of the media, and as a consequence, the public view of the President, is still very widespread in Austria. The essential reason for this is that an overview of the social and economic constellations of power which determine these decisions is, to a great extent, not passed on by the media.

NOTES

Austrian newspaper clippings 1918-1984 from the Tagblatt-Archiv (Kammer fuer Arbeiter und Angestellte, Wien, Dokumentation) and the Viktor Matejka Collection (Institut fuer Zeitgeschichte, Wien) have been used but not cited in detail in this article.

1. Karl Loewenstein quoted in Manfried Welan, "Regierung und Staasoberhaupt," Pelinka/Welan (edit.), *Geschichte der osterreichischen Bundesverfassung,* 148.

2. Hans Kelsen, Osterreichisches Staatsrecht. Ein Grundriss entwicklungs-geschichtlich dargestellt (Tuebingen: J.C.B. Mohr-Paul Siebeck, 1923),

188-192. Eric C. Kollman, "The Austrian Presidency, 1918-1958," *Austrian History Yearbook,* I (1965), 90-94.

3. Oliver Rathkolb, *Politische Propaganda der Amerikanischen Besatzungsmacht in Osterreich 1945 bis 1950 Ein Beitrag zur Geschichte des Kalten Krieges in der Presse Kulturund Rundfunkpolitik* (University of Vienna, Austria: Unpublished Ph.D. Diss., 1981)

4. Kreisky-Interview in Basta (Oct. 1984), 40 and 42; similar statements in author's interviews with Dr. Bruno Kreisky, Feb. 1, 1984.

5. Kreisky-Interview in Basta (Oct. 1984), 42.

6. Hans J. Thalberg, *Von der Kunst Osterreicher zu sein; Erinnerungen und Tagebuchnotizen* (Vienna: Bohlau, 1984), 170.

7. Walter Dean Burnham quoted in Peter Losche, *Politik in USA.* Das amerikanische Regierungs- und Gesellschaftssystem und die Praesidentschaftswohl 1976 (Opladen: Leske-Verlag + Budrich, 1977), 154.

8. Kreisky-Interview in Basta (Oct. 1984), 42.

9. Karl Renner, *Osterreich von der Ersten zur Zweiten Republik* (Vienna: Verlag der Wiener Volksbuchhandlung, 1953), 91.

10. Karl Gruber, *Ein politisches Leben.* Osterreich Weg zwischen den Diktaturen (Vienna: Fritz Molden, undated), 272.

11. Quoted in Losche, *Politik in USA,* 67

12. Adolf Scharf, *Osterreichs Erneuerung 1945-1955.* Das erste Jahrzehnt der Zweiten Republik (Vienna: Verlag der Wiener Volksbuchhandlung, 1955), 300.

13. Quoted in Edward S. Corwin, *The President. Office and Powers 1787-1957. History and Analysis of Practice and Opinion* (New York: New York University Press, 1957), 320.

14. Margaret Sterne, "The Presidents of the United States in the Eyes of Austro-Hungarian Diplomats: 1901-1913," *Austrian History Yearbook II* (1966), 167.

15. Benno Signitzer, "Die Rolle der Massenmedien in der Aussenpolitik" in Renate Kicker/Andreas Khol/Hanspeter Neuhold (edit.), 78. *Aussenpolitik und Demokratie in Osterreich.* Strukturen-Strategien-Stellungnahmen (Salzburg: Wolfgang Neugebauer, 1983), 186.

16. Vincenz Ludwig Ostry, Der maechtigste Mann der Erde (Vienna: Europa Verlag, 1968).

17. Lujo Toncic-Sorinj, *Erfullte Traeume. Kroatien-Osterreich-Europa* (Vienna: Amalthea, 1982), 298.

18. Daniel C. Hallin, "The Media, the War in Vietnam, and Political Support: A Critique of the Thesis of an Oppositional Media," *Journal of Politics-XLVI* (February 1984), 2-3.

19. Hallin, *The Media,* 22-23.

CHAPTER 5

LATIN AMERICAN PERSPECTIVES

Francisco Cuevas Cancino
and
Rene Herrera

Narrator: We are pleased to welcome you to a Forum with Ambassador Francisco Cuevas Cancino of Mexico. Ambassador Cuevas has served as ambassador to the United Nations, to UNESCO, and he's also worked in the United States on a variety of posts and assignments. He is a scholar in his own right. I thought as I met him at the airport last evening that of all the interests of the Rockefeller Foundation that paid high dividends in terms of the ultimate destiny of those who were assisted, modest assistance to El Colegio de Mexico's program in international relations must stand at or near the top of the list. Francisco was the head of the international relations program there. It has become a graduate program in international studies in every respect. But the other members included the current Mexican ambassador to Bonn, the current Mexican ambassador in Paris and the president of El Colegio today, who is perhaps Mexico's leading economist. If every time a foundation or a government agency went abroad they were able to discover four such people with whom to work, then foreign assistance would indeed be a simple matter.

Some of you may remember earlier periods in history when the appointment of a secretary general of the United Nations was discussed. In the 1960s, there were two or three leading candidates for that post and Ambassador Cuevas had considerable support from a number of leading countries. Wherever he's gone he's left a lasting imprint on the minds and feelings of those with whom he's worked. He has never hesitated to state his views on problems as forcefully and honestly as possible, but at the same time has always respected the viewpoints of other people.

He and I thought that because of the urgency and the centrality of issues of Central American policy in the world today that a discussion of some of those questions might be in the forefront of your attention. It may help us understand the differences between the Reagan administration and Mexico if we understand the Mexican approach to foreign policy. Then in the question period that follows you may want to explore more fully questions about the American presidency, the Good Neighbor policy, the Monroe Doctrine, and current policy as it affects the American presidency. It's a special honor to have Ambassador Cuevas Cancino with us this afternoon.

Ambassador Cuevas: Dr. Thompson, in such a lovely place and in such a lovely university, it is a bit idle on my part that I am very pleased to be here, but I am also very honored, not only by the people who have taken the trouble to come here this afternoon but by your invitation. I've known you now for a number of years and it is difficult to keep a friendship always half and half with admiration and respect because they have both gone together and seen that the passing of years has diminished neither one or the other.

I have the pleasure of stating perhaps the basis of what is the Mexican position in Central America. This of course raises a number of problems and I would be the first to agree that the solutions we are offering are only partial ones. But perhaps it will be a beginning for us to see if we can find a new approach that, in my own limited way, I will certainly be sure that it is heard in other quarters.

Mexico's foreign policy is a result of its history. Conceived as a shield, it looks as if designed to protect the nation that emerged from the revolution of 1910. It is therefore a cautious and defensive foreign policy, based on a series of fundamental principles such as nonintervention, self-determination, and the peaceful settlement of international disputes. If these principles protect other nations they are also a guarantee of Mexico's destiny as seen by the revolutionary government. By adopting these principles, the Mexican government tacitly accepts the nation's historic vulnerability with respect to foreign powers, especially its dominant northern neighbor.

As suited to its defense, Mexico's foreign policy carefully observes tradition and maintains continuity and consistency. Two important variables define the need for a basic understanding with the United States and the maintenance of local internal order; these are the boundaries within which any foreign policy may be exercised.

The interplay of these two forces makes it very difficult for Mexico to reconcile the defense of her national interest vis-a-vis Central America with that of the United States. In this region one could characterize the constant dilemma of Mexican foreign policy as the reconciliation between two widely different objectives: the maintenance of her nonintervention line, and the avoidance of contradictory actions towards the United States, given Mexico's high degree of dependence in economic matters on the U.S.

As history provides a solid base, let us examine the past in order to understand Mexico's present position with respect to Central America. Let us fix our attention on the decade of the sixties, when the emergence of a socialist regime in Cuba and its subsequent alliance with the Soviet Union abruptly changed the pattern of what we might term classic inter-american relations.

With regard to Cuba, Mexico consistently opposed intervention, defending the right of the Cuban people to self-determination. In various meetings of foreign ministers, within the Organization of American States (OAS)—at Punta del Este principally—Mexico opposed the exclusion of Cuba from the inter-american system. Later on, in 1964, Mexico voted against the resolution, calling on all members of the OAS to break off relations with Cuba. Not only did Mexico oppose such resolution, but even decided not to implement it, even if it was legally binding under the Rio Treaty. The fact that those other countries (Chile, Bolivia, and Uruguay), which still maintained relations, broke their ties with the Cuban govenment in response to the mandatory resolution, shows the length to which Mexico was prepared to go in matters affecting the Caribbean. To complete the picture it should be added that one year later, in 1965, and this time with respect to the political crisis in the Dominican Republic, Mexico voted against the creation of an inter-american peace force and introduced a resolution that the U.S. expeditionary force should leave the Dominican Republic.

A similar case which is also important as an indicator of Mexican vital interests comes to my mind. At the time of the so-called "missile crisis" in October of 1962, the council of the OAS unanimously approved a resolution supporting measures "including the use of armed force" in order to assure the withdrawal of the Soviet missiles from Cuba. The Mexican delegation, together with those of Brazil and Bolivia, introduced a reservation to the effect that this resolution should not be taken as a justification for an armed attack on Cuba. Even if these three countries approved military measures against a neighboring state, they clearly opposed a blank check to invade Cuba and overthrow the revolutionary government. Mexico, Brazil, and Bolivia opposed the conversion of Cuba into a military base of an extra-continental power—which is one of the outstanding tenets of the inter-american system—at the same time opposed intervention in the internal affairs of an American republic; that is, they opposed the utilization of the crisis as an excuse for a "definitive" action against the Cuban revolution. The distinction between a regional and a global confrontation remained explicit.

Another experience is relevant to the regional approach which today concerns us. This has to do with the resolutions approved in 1967 by the Organization Latinoamericana de Solidaridad (OLAS), an organization created in that year under the auspices of the Castro government to foster revolutions in Latin America. On that occasion, and confronting Cuba, Mexico also came out in defense of the principle of nonintervention. It is interesting to recall the statement made then by the Mexican minister of foreign affairs: ". . .there can be no doubt that the Mexican government disapproves the resolutions voted in Havana earlier this year. . .Mexico has tried very hard to understand Cuba and to defend the principles of nonintervention and self-determination which allow its people to freely modify its institutions and its form of government; but if in violation of these principles there is an attempt to disregard our free self-determination, intervening in matters which only Mexico has a right to decide, we will have to take adequate measures for our own defense."

In 1967 an advisor to the Committee on Foreign Affairs of the United States Senate, Pat Holt, made a statement which should be quoted as part of the present analysis: ". . .It is worth the trouble to note the apparent paradox that Mexico is the Latin American country with which the United States has maintained the best relations and also the one which most inflexibly resists all types of collective action against Cuba. Even more, Mexico is the only country in Latin America which has, as a matter of principle, refused to sign an agreement guaranteeing United States investments and yet is one of the most attractive places for United States investments. It is the only Latin American country which does not have an agreement for military assistance with the United States (again as a matter of principle) and yet is one of the few Latin American countries where there is unquestionably civil control of the armed forces."

One year after posing this paradox, Holt himself undertook to explain it: "It is somewhat strange for the United States, but it appears that Mexico has a special dispensation to dissent with us. If the Mexicans oppose in the OAS something which the Department of State strongly desires, everyone takes it in stride, no one is upset, and we remain friends with the Mexicans."

We have perhaps reached the core of the matter, a sort of tacit understanding between Mexico and the United States by means of which

Washington accepts Mexico's dissent from U.S. policy under certain conditions: that it is a fundamental matter of Mexico, and that, even more important, it does not fundamentally affect U.S. foreign policy. The counterpart is that Mexico engages itself to cooperate with the U.S. in everything which is truly fundamental for it. The way in which the "missile crisis" was handled gives an excellent example of the principles above. If I may emphasize it once again: Mexico approved the measures which assured the dismantling of the Soviet missile bases in Cuba, including the use of armed force, but made sure that this action against extra-continental aggression could not be taken as a justification for action destined to destroy the Cuban revolutionary government.

Let us now come to present-day events in Central America. Even if we can find some similarities with those that occurred during the sixties, they are not exactly alike and each has its own peculiarities. It is true that the eighties point to the resurgence of the cold war; however, important changes in the international and regional structures appear. First, a number of countries are stronger than twenty years ago. Second, Mexico possesses a concrete instrument of economic power and political influence because oil, undoubtedly, is an element that vastly upgrades international influence. Third, there appears to exist a regional atmosphere which is more conducive to solidarity and cooperation among the countries in the Caribbean. Perhaps this new atmosphere has been at the root of the complementary energy pact between Venezuela and Mexico that provides the wherewithal of the oil consumed by the rest of the countries in the region. We can also perceive a heightened consciousness—at least among countries with civil governments such as Colombia, Costa Rica, Venezuela, and Mexico—for the need to strengthen ties through economic cooperation and political solidarity in the face of a menacing world economy. Perhaps we can interpret all these trends in the sense that the noninterventionist stand of Mexico will be stronger; we can also easily conclude that in such a stand, it will have the support of other Latin American countries.

Let me repeat for clarity's sake that the constant dilemma of Mexican foreign policy has been the conciliation of those two main objectives that have not changed with the passage of time: its noninterventionist line and a kind of implementation that will not overly contradict the United States. The first objective is usually defined in Mexican terms as the continuity and consistency of its foreign policy; the second (given the importance and the complexity of the bilateral relationship with her neighbor to the north, and its high degree of economic dependence on the United States) is tacitly but constantly kept in mind.

United States Intervention in Central America

At the end of the seventies Mexico's foreign policy has a complete set of new cards in Central America: the fall of Somoza, the victorious Sandinist revolution, the Hondurean-Salvadorean war that virtually stopped the Central America Common Market, the consequent civil war in El Salvador, and the racial overtones of the Guatemala anti-guerrilla war.

The Mexican government, acting in accordance with its revolutionary ideals and with a close knowledge of what is happening in Central America, takes the view that there are no alternatives, in the long run, to revolutionary change. The crisis, says the Mexican govenment, arises from the unravelling of political models imposed by force (on more than one occasion with United States support) and not so much from imperialist plans supposedly approved by Havana and Moscow. According to the Mexican view, intervention by the United States, direct or indirect, would not suppress this revolutionary option. On the contrary, it will thwart the natural political development of the region and make the inevitable revolution much more cruel and more extreme. In addition, Mexico considers that the option of revolutionary change is as valid for Central America as it was for Mexico in 1910. Furthermore, Mexico's great preoccupation is that a regional war could arise in its own backyard, especially one created by the artificial necessity of reasserting American hegemonic power in a part of the world where no basic confrontation exists. Such a turn of events would create a profound and permanent instability in Mexico itself and with its relations with the United States. This basic lack of understanding would ruin the possibility of further developing its economic relations with the United States.

Since 1979 Mexico has aimed at a negotiated solution to the regional crisis in Central America. Of course its perception is influenced by its new eminence as one of the great oil producing countries, but principally (as it was clear to all thinking people) because the Central American crisis could affect vital national interests. What the Mexican government desires—let us not forget that the mystique of the revolution is still alive—is to continue to implement its development programs without having a wide focus of armed tension next door. If such tensions were ever to evolve into a Central American war, Mexico's vision of the problem would have to change; it would, much to its distress, be forced to consider a new defense policy. Its negative implications on the development objectives of a fast growing population would be catastrophic. Let us remember that even under the most optimistic considerations, Mexico will reach over one hundred million inhabitants at the turn of the century.

In economic terms, this Central American belligerency at the international level would be the greatest catastrophe for the Mexican revolutionary government. It would signify a diversion of resources from badly underdeveloped areas; it would weaken the traditional political class, forcing it to share the development strategies with the military sector and putting an end to over forty years of civilian rule; furthermore, it would initiate a policy of close association with U.S. corporate and security interests and would lead to the failure of present efforts to introduce pluralism into its political system. Present-day efforts, destined to incorporate political opponents by institutionalizing the participation of diverse ideological forces in the electoral process, would become useless. Security considerations would prevail over domestic political modernization. Political strife would render futile democratization and would provoke serious confrontations in Mexican society. Then, and only then, the crisis predicted for Mexico by supporters of the so-called domino theory would become a reality; only in this case it would be precisely by following the prescription of those that supposedly desire to avoid it.

As the Mexican political class fully realizes this possibility, it is steadfast in its insistence of a negotiated solution to the Central American crisis.

The Mexican position in Central America, as it appears since 1979, seems to U.S. circles as aggressive and radical; it has thus become the object of increased concern. Many regard it as an expression of international activism, sustained by the new petroleum wealth, and aimed at gaining a position of power in a region historically considered part of the North American domain. Only exceptionally in the past, very exceptionally and in a very restricted manner, had Mexico dared to intervene in Central America against, or even better in alliance with, the U.S. One occasion was the Diaz-Taft agreement that achieved peace at the turn of the century; the other was the military aid that President Calles sent precisely to Augusto Sandino to fight American marines in Nicaragua in 1925.

United States policymakers still find the Mexican attitude confusing and exasperating. Their irritation grew as they found the Mexican attitude being followed by other Latin countries involved in Central America. Thus it becomes easy for Washington to argue that Mexico's foreign policy is purely motivated by an emotional anti-Americanism; or, even better, that it reflects the need to reaffirm the "macho" public image of a country unsure of its roots.

The open Mexican support for the Sandinist government, its uninterrupted friendly ties with Cuba, and its joint declaration with France recognizing the Salvadorean revolutionary forces (August 1981) provoked consternation on the part of the U.S., as well as open criticism from other Latin American countries. As a consequence, Mexico suffered strong pressure from the U.S. and from other Latin American countries (particularly Venezuela, Colombia and Costa Rica). This pressure, however, did not succeed in affecting Mexico's Central American policy. It continued to work closely with the Sandinistas and to seek, in accordance with the Cuban government and Salvadorean rebel leaders, possible routes of negotiation with the United States.

During this period, when the world oil glut produced dramatic declines in revenues for the oil-producing countries, a long avoided crisis burst into Mexico. President de la Madrid, who occupied the presidency in December 1982, found everything, including foreign policy, in decline. Under the sign of financial crisis, a new strategy was launched. It consisted in limiting Mexico's vulnerability in the pretension that the economic situation of a country does not alter its foreign policy. After all, it was said, the principles upon which Mexican foreign policy rests are unchangeable. Why should they now suffer deviations because the country has become a heavy debtor?

Mexican presence in Central American affairs has not diminished. Conflicts have been steadily growing in the area all during 1983, but the Mexican prescription has been to redouble its efforts towards a negotiated settlement. This objective is considered important enough to ride over the strenuous resistance put against it by the United States.

The new strategy as developed by President de la Madrid seems to comprise the following steps:

1) To restore a regional consensus as a means of reducing the foreign and bellicose external pressures exercised in the region both by the United States and by Cuba;

2) At the same time, to reduce Mexican unilateral responsibility in the Central American crisis area, taking instead joint action with other interested Latin American republics;

3) Thus, and consequently, using the Contadora Group (as a multilateral and informational group) to avoid acting single-handedly in the Central American crisis;

4) To use the same Contadora Group over Cuba and Nicaragua in order to moderate their positions;

5) To use the same Contadora Group as an influential element in the formation of North American public opinion; and

6) To avoid the OAS, since this organization no longer universally represents both the Americas.

Let me finish with a definition of the way I see the role of Mexico with regard to the present-day Central American crisis. Let us accept, as a working hypothesis, that Mexico's economic crisis will not substantially affect its stand. Let us also accept that its different approach to the crisis will not basically affect its bilateral relations with the United States. That said, I would hazard three fundamental and related conclusions. Firstly, that Mexico, through indirect channels like the Contadora Group, will continue to maintain the full application of the principles of self-determination and nonintervention for all of Central America. Second, that Mexico will diplomatically seek a political solution through negotiations between all the parties directly involved. Third, that Mexico will dedicate growing efforts to persuade American public opinion that Mexico's dissent with respect to Central America does not touch the basic interests of the U.S. And fourth, to preach at all times that the clock of history cannot be put back, and that all democratic countries should support the revolutionary forces as genuine instruments of democratization.

Mexico is fully aware that its vital national interests are intimately linked to the peaceful settlement of the conflicts in Central America. Mexico also knows that the Contadora Group, whose aim is to achieve a negotiated settlement of the Central American crisis, respecting the identity of every one of the five republics concerned, constitutes the limits of its present Central American commitment. It does not even wish to consider a military sort of commitment and will do everything in its power to avoid it.

I have the impression I've made a partial, though perhaps an imperfect, synthesis of how we stand and I'll be at your complete disposal to give as true answers as possible to your questions or give any more information that I can.

Question: Ambassador, has the Mexican government been doing anything to reduce the very rapid population growth there? It seems to me to be very dangerous for both political and economic reasons.

Ambassador Cuevas: We have launched a campaign that is now about ten years old. The government is rather pleased with the results. When we started we had something like 3.2 or 3.4 growth, now it's down to 2.6, perhaps or 2.8. This is why the optimistic projections of which I spoke will be that we will reach about 100 or 105 million, but it should level off at that and if that is the case then we can meet the rest of the twenty-first century with optimism. But we couldn't agree more; we are fully conscious that it would be a disastrous thing that the population should continue to grow. An energetic campaign of family planning has been going on and it is still being implemented.

Question: I think all of us would agree with the idea of nonintervention. But how do you tell when something is truly a revolution arising from all of the people in contrast to something that is being stimulated from an outside foreign source? And how does Mexico look at the influence of Cuba, which is far-flung around the globe at the present time and must be supported from somewhere? Certainly they're not raising that sort of support from within their own islands. How do you square that with your position of nonintervention such as the Contadora Group suggests?

Ambassador Cuevas: I'm perfectly aware of what you say about Cuba because I know that the U.S. government believes that the Soviet Union is putting in an enormous amount of money in the Caribbean. As far as our immediate means of knowledge is concerned, we have had extensive talks with the Cuban government. In fact, just at the beginning of this negotiating procedure of the Contadora Group during the last year, Carlos Rafael Rodriquez, the number two ideologue in the Cuban government, went to Mexico. We had extensive talks, and they assured us that what they want is acceptable. They had advised their friends in Salvador not to push things to the extreme, and they are for controlling, we understood, with definite means, what the Nicaraguans are doing to export revolution. In other words, they do not believe that it is in their interest to upset the whole Central American balance as it is today because, I believe, they are not willing to take more commitments.

Now of course you are absolutely right in that any revolution today with the presence of a hegemonic power like the Soviet Union—which certainly takes advantage of any weakening in the composition or in the setup of the democratic world—is indeed taking advantage of it. And it is very difficult to know where to draw the line. I have pondered a lot about it and in fact since I had the occasion to give a lecture on the Good Neighbor policy I asked myself the same question. In the lecture, I quoted an element that perhaps could give us some inkling of what to do.

There was an exchange of communications that occurred in 1935 between Roosevelt and Morgenthau, not Hans but Henry, the U.S. secretary of the treasury at the time. Now the United States Congress had approved the Silver Act. Many countries, among them China, found themselves in very difficult circumstances because their coinage was more valuable as silver, and therefore, it was absolved by the United States. So Morgenthau passed on to Roosevelt the complaints of some American missionaries in China, and Roosevelt's reply offers those vistas that perhaps could give us today, I think, an indication of what a Mexican is thinking. "Those missionaries," said Roosevelt, "belong to a system that has exploited China and that implies the orthodox application of a monetary policy that has nothing to offer to China and that has no place under the New Deal. China has been a haven for those who are equal to the moneylenders that Jesus expelled from the temple. Many years and a few revolutions will be necessary to break their hold on China. And it seems to me that the interests of the United States are not those of the moneylenders and that our policies should be to allow that country to stand on its own feet." Now as I look at the rather dismal episode of what happened in China, as far as the U.S. taking the brunt of what really was intervention of European powers—because if any Western power had a clean slate in Chinese affairs it was the U.S.—I think that perhaps it would be worthwhile to try this sentiment instead of acting, and acting violently, in defense of interests in situations which are not your doing. But I realize it is a very difficult matter.

Question: Following on that and realizing that there would be tremendous problems in Central America were there nothing but ocean where all Communist states now exist, including Cuba, one is still forced to raise the question, what kind of settlement do you really want to negotiate? In other words, there is a danger that the emphasis be simply on the negotiating process and victory achieved simply if we negotiate, whereas I think we also need to look at the settlement itself. Have you, or has Mexico, any reasonably clear picture yet of what kind of negotiation it hopes to come up with?

Ambassador Cuevas: I would say that it would be limiting the revolutionary forces to Nicaragua, that we would allow the government of El Salvador to impose its rule, and we would, as you have already, consolidate the holdings in the rest of Central America to make it impossible for any more adventures to take place. What I am suggesting is not too different from what Mr. Linowitz suggested a little while ago.

But I have the impression that the position taken in Washington is rather to upset the Nicaraguan government and to stop where we were. Perhaps it is possible now.

In Latin America a different approach is taken to Communist regimes in other parts of the world, and those regimes are therefore allowed to evolve. Deng of China received very well in the West and he says, "Well, yes, of course I'm a Marxist but I want contacts and support of the West," and he gets them. And Mr. Bishop comes here and you see what happens. We should, shall I say, allow the boiling point to be all equal and allow countries which are Communist to become Yugoslavias, which would not be too bad as partners.

Question: You bring to mind what I felt was the greatest tragedy in our foreign policy within my recent memory and that was the Allende affair. I wept, literally, when that happened having worked for a year in Colombia and dealt with Latin America. I felt that here was the beginning of just what you were speaking of, Allende, and then to learn that we were so actively involved in bringing about his downfall really crushed me. Now am I misinterpreting that in your view? Have we learned anything from that experience or is my impression wrong?

Ambassador Cuevas: I do not think that the policy has changed. The idea that it is still possible to bring down the revolutionary government in Latin America by the use of force I think is still prevalent.

Question: How can that be changed?

Ambassador Cuevas: Again one of the conclusions I was putting forward in the speech on the Good Neighbor policy is that the responsibilities of a great power are great indeed, because only the great power itself can set limits to its action and therefore it's up to you. Fortunately, as Carlos Fuentes said in his speech at Harvard, "We are in a democracy and are hurt and you are able to influence your government; but we are in your hands." It is very little that the Mexican can do except speak to you.

Question: I've heard that speech of Carlos Fuentes and it was marvelously given, an expressive interpretation. One of the aspects that has intrigued me, and he alluded to it a little bit, is that the United States holds up our own revolution as a model, which is that very shortly after the fighting died down we became a democracy. We elected governments, and there weren't very many armed interventions in the process. We see revolutions, and we see one side winning a revolution, but then we don't see democracy or we don't see what seems to be democracy to us anyway. I wonder if you could comment on that. It seems to give us a lot of trouble that revolutions don't do what we would like to have them do. What they do to us, in a sense, is bring us a sense of democracy.

Ambassador Cuevas: May I refer, since it has been the bicentennial of Bolivar, to his famous speech in Angostura when he outlined what the composition of Columbia should be? He posed to himself the question of how are the people coming out of centuries of colonialism with such great limitations going to be governed. And he makes comparisons very favorably to your own nation. He said, "Of course, such principles can work well in the United States where they have all the institutions and they could easily go from there to a national government, but for us it is virtually impossible. So how should we avoid the extremes of anarchy and tyrannical government? We'll have to look for something which works in each country." Now of course sometimes I get very displeased when I read, in this case in the British press, rather scathing comments about the lack of democracy that exists in Mexico. According to the normal patterns of democracy, well, you are quite right, it's a main party that is supported by the government. You don't know where the party ends and the government starts. But it works. Many of the basic liberties in Mexico exist and something which is basically good is done for the majority of people. So I think we should ask you to consider that it is not a set standard—democracy is not ABC—it has to change from country to country. In America, as my Brazilian colleague would say, how can you speak of tyrannical, military government in a country like Brazil? It's against the Brazilian way of thinking. So please examine each case on its own and perhaps you will find that it's not so different in its achievements as the ideal could be.

Question: What do you see as the implications for Mexico should the country default on the national debt?

Ambassador Cuevas: I don't think that is realistic question. In fact I was privileged to be at the side of the minister of finance during the visit he paid to the London banks. It is clear that the decision has been taken at the highest level and I believe it's going to be implemented. We're going to pay. The whole setup is to enable the policies of the international monetary fund to take place. We have already renegotiated our debt in order to put it mainly in long terms and with reasonable periods of defaulting which are already accepted, but we have not considered the possibility of defaulting. And in the recent Caracas meeting Mexico was the main force opposed to creating what was called the cartel of the debtor nations, probably the essential element in avoiding it. It is not within our political comprehension.

Question: Is it possible at this stage, since the development with the present administration in Washington won't change, that there can be a regional conference of the Latin American nations and the United States to get together and enlighten the administration, and present new viewpoints to the administration? Is it possible that we have that much influence or can generate that much influence?

Ambassador Cuevas: I don't think it is possible. The latest contacts I've had in what I know have taken place in Mexico do not indicate that possibility. We are in a way suffering from our own misbehavior because the Organization of American States was created exactly with that purpose but we have misused it, we have left it undecided, we have said one way or the other that it was never meant to make political decisions, which of course it was. And now what we need the instrument, it is no longer there. For instance, I am fully convinced that actually in the Grenada case it was necessary. The country was fast going into anarchy put it would have been very different if it had been taken at the level of an inter-American system. It would have none of the blame.

Somehow, somewhere, we must start rebuilding the OAS. It is an indispensable element for the creating of an inter-american policy and for free negotiating between the all-powerful United States and the other Latin American nations.

Question: Wouldn't it be in our best interests to pursue that policy?

Ambassador Cuevas: Of course. It would be an excellent thing.

Narrator: We thank you very much for being with us. I might mention one thing. We are especially pleased that the publisher of most of the works of the Miller Center is with us, Jed Lyons of the University Press of America. We, at the Miller Center, are enormously pleased that we've had a joint publishing understanding with the University Press of America. We hope to continue that good relationship.

I know I speak for all of you in thanking Ambassador Cuevas for his calm and reasoned presentation, his willingness to state fully his own position and that of his government, his desire also to have your point of view and hopefully to be in some way a bridge between those of us who may have other views and he and his colleagues who work in the region to achieve its best interests. His young colleague, Rene Herrera assisted with the paper. Thank you so much for being with us.

CHAPTER 6

CONCEPTS OF LEADERSHIP: NEHRU, THE PEACEMAKER

T.N. Kaul

Narrator: This is a jointly sponsored Forum by the Committee on the Individual In Society and the Miller Center. We've had a couple of these Forums and discussions on leadership which is of course a concern of the Miller Center but also is a major concern of the Committee on the Individual In Society. We are especially pleased as well that some of the faculty most concerned with India, not least Walter Hauser who is Mr. India at the University of Virginia, could be here. David Shannon has been in India on many occasions and has had strong interest in that area as well as others. It would be nice if Professor Khare could introduce our speaker.

Professor Khare: Thank you, Ken. It is my proud privilege to welcome Mr. T.N. Kaul to the University and to the committee and to the Center for Advanced Studies, which is the sponsor for this committee, and the Faulkner House with Ken's gracious hospitality.

Mr. Kaul hardly needs any introduction, particularly to the Indianists. He has been a scholar in his own right and he has been one of the most prominent administrative service officers in India. He has held some of the most important appointments in government affairs since independence. Immediately after independence and before that he was in the Indian civil service. He joined the Indian civil service in 1937 and he served until India became independent in 1947. From 1947 to 1949 he was first secretary in the Indian embassy in Moscow; from 1949 to 1950 he was first secretary in the Indian embassy in Washington; from 1950 to 1954 he was minister to the People's Republic of China during which time he negotiated the Treaty of the Five Principles of Peaceful Coexistence (Pancasila); from 1954 to 1957 he was in the foreign office in New Delhi; from 1958 to 1960 he was ambassador to Iran; from 1960 to 1962 he was deputy and acting high commissioner of London; from 1962 to 1966 he was ambassador to Moscow; from 1966 to 1972, he was Foreign Secretary in New Delhi; and from 1972 to 1976 ambassador to Washington; from 1976 to 1977 he was president of the Indian Council of Cultural Relations; and from 1980 onwards he has been on the executive board of UNESCO in Paris. He holds of course numerous scholarly as well as public welfare and public speaking appointments; he gave the Nehru Memorial Lecture at the University of London.

He has written several books: *Diplomacy in War and Peace* in 1979; *India, China and Indochina* in 1980; *The Kissinger Years* published in New Delhi in 1980; and the latest one, *Reminiscences: Discreet and Indiscreet* again from New Delhi in 1982. So it is indeed a whole parade of the later part of the century. We are pleased and honored to have Mr. Kaul among ourselves. He will be talking on Nehru, the peacemaker, this afternoon. Mr. Ambassador.

Ambassador Kaul: Thank you very much. I am indeed grateful to the Miller Center and the committee for giving me this opportunity to exchange ideas with you. I do not believe in teaching others but I do believe in learning from others. So this is really an exchange of ideas and I hope you will forgive me if I speak as a "liberated" diplomat, freely and frankly among friends, and won't mind my frankness.

The subject is a vast one—the concept of leadership, particularly with reference to Jawaharlal Nehru and his role as a peacemaker. My discourse may throw light, indirectly at least, on the Indian view of the U.S. Presidency. I think it is perhaps just as well to point out at the very outset that your President, for instance, is in some ways very different from our President who is more like a British monarch—the constitutional head of a state. He has more ceremonial duties than policymaking ones. But our prime minister, who is the leader of the largest parliamentary party elected in our country during the general elections based on adult suffrage and secret vote, is perhaps closer to your idea of a President. The difference is that your President is only in some ways answerable to Congress and has more powers than our prime minister has in a parliamentary democracy where the prime minister is answerable to Parliament and can only hold power as long as he or she commands the majority in Parliament.

But Nehru was a unique prime minister in the sense that he was the first prime minister, as well as the foreign minister, immediately after independence. He and Gandhi were two major leaders who successfully launched a nonviolent struggle for India's independence from British rule. His background was responsible for many of his ideas. He had been educated in Harrow and Cambridge; he had been influenced by Fabian socialism to some extent; he had visited Brussels and attended the meeting of the League Against Imperialism in 1927; and then he visited Moscow that year along with his father. That attracted him somewhat to the idealistic aspects of Marxism but he refused to become a camp follower or a fellow traveler and criticized the League Against Imperialism for their dictatorial ways and means of controlling the movements in other countries. Ultimately he was expelled by them.

But when he came back to India he was groping for some way out of the contradiction that he saw between the British ideas of democracy and how the British were behaving in India. This upset him, shocked him, particularly with all the poverty and misery of the millions of peasants in India. He was itching for some action. He could not fit himself into the mold of the upper middle-class liberals and he refused to collaborate with the British government who made many offers to him. He found in Gandhi perhaps a way out of this impasse; Gandhi's civil disobedience movement attracted him because Nehru was mainly a man of action.

Will Durant, the American philosopher, once asked, "What is the meaning of life for you?" Nehru said, "As long as I am active in the pursuit of my goals and ideals, life has a meaning for me, whether I achieve those goals and ideals or not. It is the effort that counts." And this was in line with the teachings of the Bhagavad-Gita which in the second chapter says the same thing, "Karmane Vadhikar aste, mate Phaleshu Kadacana" (One has the right only to work and not to its fruit).

So there was Nehru, the idealist, the revolutionary, the follower of Gandhi, and yet not quite believing in Gandhi's philosophy of treating the landlord and the industrialist as the trustee of the workers, of the peasants. He did not agree with Gandhi's philosophy of village self-sufficiency. He believed in the policy of industrialization and large river valley schemes and power projects and exploring the frontiers of science and knowledge for the benefit of the common man. And even before independence he had an idea of a planned economy; he was the chairman of the National Planning Committee which had been appointed by the Congress party. His idea was to inject a social and economic content into the concept of political independence. Political independence alone for him was not enough. He did not agree with Gandhi entirely. He agreed that violence was a bad thing but he also said, "Violence is bad but slavery is far worse." For him, means were important but not more important than the ends. For Gandhi, means were sometimes even more important than ends.

I'm mentioning this difference between Gandhi and Nehru because I think it was important in post-independence India. Nevertheless, I think the two complimented each other. And so far as foreign international affairs are concerned, Gandhi let Nehru have the upper hand in drafting various resolutions for the Congress party even before independence. In fact he once said "he is our Englishman" because he used to draft all the resolutions.

Gandhi was against the partition of India and he gave his life for it; he was assassinated by a fanatic Hindu. But the Congress party with Nehru, Vallabhai Patel, Maulana Azad and others thought that partition was the lesser of two evils; they would rather have a partitioned but independent India than a united India under foreign domination. For Gandhi the unity of India was something far more important than for Nehru and his colleagues.

Gandhi let them have their way. He said, "All right, you want an independent state, even if it means a truncated India." But Gandhi's assassination by a fanatic Hindu was a very great shock for Nehru. He said in a broadcast on the night of Gandhi's assassination, "The light has gone out of our lives." After that, I think, he fulfilled Gandhi's prediction. Gandhi had said, "We may speak a different language but language is not any bar to the union of hearts and after my death Nehru will speak my language." These were almost prophetic words because Nehru, after Gandhi's death, became more realistic, more pragmatic, more practical. The old revolutionary fire in Nehru, although you could see sparks of it now and again, was brought more down to earth. He tried at the same time to formulate the foreign policy of India and the internal policy of India in accordance with the golden ideals that he and Gandhi had enunciated during the freedom struggle.

It was not as if Nehru became the leader because Gandhi had nominated him as his "political heir." Nehru was the one man, I think, who inspired particuarly my generation of Indians with his enthusiasm, his fire, his idealism, his convictions and beliefs in social justice as well as economic growth, and notions of equality among all the people irrespective of caste, creed, or sex.

But as time went on I think Nehru had to face realities surrounding the world, and particularly India, after World War II. There was the Cold War that set in. In 1927, in 1940, and again on the eve of independence, in his famous broadcast on All-India Radio on the sixth of September, 1946, he had said, "We will not be the allies of any other state however powerful that it may be. We shall not get involved in the rivalry, the ideological or military rivalry or hostility, of the two power blocs. It's bad enough; it has led to wars in the past, it can lead to wars again. We stand for peace." That is why he enunciated the policy of nonalignment which was not to get involved in the military alliances or the great power rivalries of the two power blocs that came into existence almost immediately after World War II.

In the beginning Nehru was criticized by, among others, John Foster Dulles, who called nonalignment immoral. But as time went on more and more countries that became independent saw in this policy of nonalignment a way of maintaining their independence of thought, action, and judgment in any given situation. Nonalignment was not a policy of neutrality or neutralism as the Western media often call it even now, and as Henry Kissinger called it, deliberately perhaps. It was a policy of judging each issue on its merits, as it arose, as it affected our own national interests and the larger interests of world peace.

Peace was a passion with Nehru because he believed that unless there was peace in the world, peace in India, and peace in the developing countries, it would be impossible to have economic or social development to restructure our society or economy. And, therefore, he worked passionately for the peaceful settlement of international disputes and for relaxation of international tensions. Although India was militarily weak and economically backward, he succeeded, particularly during the fifties, in acting as a sort of bridge, as a catalytic agent, to reduce international tensions and to resolve peacefully some of the conflicts that arose.

You have an example of that in the case of the Korean crisis in 1950. Nehru played a very significant part in trying to bring about a cease-fire in Korea with the result that both sides asked India to be the chairman of the Neutral Nations Repatriation Commission in Korea.

Then again in the case of Indochina, Nehru called a conference of the Six Colombo Powers, all nonaligned except Pakistan. And they played a significant role in the success of the Indochina Geneva agreements which brought about a ceasefire. As a result of this, India was asked to be the chairman of the International Supervisory Commissions in the three states of Indochina. I happened to be the chairman of the commission on Vietnam. It was not an easy task but I think we were able, at least, to prevent the situation from worsening in the early years. Playing a catalytic role, the international commission prevented war, for some years at least, from escalating.

Then again in the Suez crisis in 1956, Nehru played a very important role. I'm glad that on that issue John Foster Dulles agreed with Nehru on most things and we were together able to persuade both the U.K. and France to withdraw their troops from the Suez Canal.

Again in the Congo crisis, it was not merely that Nehru talked of peace but he was not afraid of shouldering the responsibilities of maintaining peace in the peacekeeping force under the U.N. in Congo. India was, I think, the major contributing force in keeping the peace there.

These are some of the examples of Nehru's passion for peace and his efforts to bring about some kind of an understanding between the two rival blocs and to play a constructive and positive role to prevent war from spreading.

In the United Nations, India under Nehru's leadership played again a very vital role in the process of decolonization from 1960 onwards which resulted in the liberation and independence of almost one hundred countries. And the nonaligned movement also spread. In 1961 at the Belgrade Summit there were only twenty-five members. But in the seventh summit held in New Delhi last year there were one hundred and one members. They do not count for much in the game of power politics, in a military or economic sense, but I think as a moral force for peace, for disarmament, for the struggle against racism, they have played a very important role.

In the field of disarmament Nehru was the first statesman to propose in 1954 the idea of bringing about a general and complete disarmament by international safeguards and control. After both America and the Soviet Union had acquired the nuclear bomb, he said we were living in a "balance of terror," and that this mad race must be stopped. He was the first world statesman to propose nuclear disarmament in 1954. I must say that in spite of the fact that India had the nuclear capability as early as 1958, 1962, and 1964, Nehru did not approve the idea of having a nuclear explosion even for peaceful purposes at that time.

I remember having a talk with Dr. Howi Bhabba who was the head of our Atomic Energy Commission at that time. He told me that we could have had a nuclear explosion within six months. This was around 1958, 1960, 1962, but Nehru did not give him the green light. Of course China exploded its first nuclear bomb in October 1964. And still we waited for another ten years before we had our first nuclear peaceful underground explosion in 1974. I am mentioning this only to show that in spite of the fact that we had the nuclear capability, Nehru did not want to proliferate nuclear weapons and he had hoped that perhaps if India refrained from doing it, it would have a deterrent influence, not only on the other non-nuclear powers but also on the nuclear powers themselves. That did not happen.

The Nuclear Nonproliferation Treaty of 1968 was a retrograde step because it gave the monopoly of nuclear technology only to the nuclear weapon powers; it imposed controls and safeguards on the non-nuclear weapon powers, but not on the nuclear weapon powers. The result was that in spite of the lip service that was paid to nuclear disarmament in the preamble of the treaty, we find that the nuclear weapon powers, particularly the two superpowers and China and France, have increased further their nuclear arsenals. That is why India has not signed the Nuclear Nonproliferation Treaty.

We are facing a threat from China. And now if Pakistan which, according to American experts, has already exploded a nuclear device that they got from China, there will be a reaction in India. I don't know what the government will do but this is a serious situation. If Nehru had been alive today, I think he would have launched a very strong worldwide campaign in favor of nuclear disarmament. It is really unthinkable that there are fifty thousand nuclear weapons in the world today and the two superpowers alone have the capacity to destroy not only each other but the whole world fourteen times over. The mutually assured destruction plan is aptly called MAD. I think the capacity to destroy the world once is bad enough but is there a need to destroy the world fourteen times over? Anyway I'm leaving that thought with you.

So far as Nehru's policy toward other powers is concerned, particularly the two superpowers (I don't like the word superpower because I think it attaches too much importance to military and economic power, but that is the usual language we use), he tried first and foremost to develop very close relations with the United States of America because he genuinely admired the advance in science and technology, the innovative spirit, the research and development of this great country. But he would not accept dictation from anybody. When he visited the United States in 1949, I, a mere first secretary in the embassy in Washington, asked him, "Sir, why don't you import wheat from the United States on concessional terms to tide over our present difficulties?" He said, "I want India to be self-reliant and self-sufficient and I will not accept any kind of aid if it has strings attached to it." He thought we would be self-sufficient in the next two or three years. That didn't happen but that was his hope and that was his effort. Although the U.S. administration tried to attract him by all kinds of offers with strings, he would not accept them.

Then came the U.S. military aid agreement with Pakistan in 1954. Although it was meant to stem the tide of international Communism, we felt that Pakistan would use this military aid against India and not against international Communism. There was an exchange of letters between President Eisenhower and Mr. Nehru, and President Eisenhower assured him that these weapons would not be used against India. That assurance proved wrong as we found in 1965 and 1971. But in spite of that Nehru tried his best to improve relations with the United States.

At the same time he tried to improve relations with China because he felt that friendly relations between two great Asian countries like India and China would not only be beneficial to them but would strengthen peace and cooperation in the whole world. I had the honor of negotiating the Pancasila agreement of 1954, as Dr. Khare told you, and in the preamble of that agreement the five principles of peaceful coexistence were laid down. We had hoped that China would abide by them. The one great shock that Nehru suffered in his life was the violation of these five principles by China in the massive invasion of India in 1962. That really gave a very serious setback to him both physically and otherwise. But I must say to his credit that another leader in his position would have resigned or gone under, but he treated the military defeat of India in 1962 as an opportunity to unite the nation and to strengthen our defenses which had been neglected from 1954 to 1962. He did succeed in strengthening the feeling of unity in India without creating a feeling of chauvinism or anti-China feeling. Although there were many chauvinistic elements in India who were rabidly against China, he did not break diplomatic relations with China.

Similarly in relation to Pakistan, in spite of Pakistan's attack on Kashmir in 1947 to 1948, when Kashmir acceded to India under the Indian Independence Act, Nehru did send troops to Kashmir, Indian troops, with the blessings of Gandhi. And they succeeded in driving the invader out of the capital. The Pakistani raiders were very near there, out up to Baramulla, Palan and beyond. And Nehru, prompted partly by Mountbatten, partly by his own desire to find a peaceful settlement of this problem, sent a complaint to the United Nations against aggression by Pakistan in Kashmir. This was an act of faith in the United Nations at that time, but unfortunately the issue became complex because the great powers, particularly the U.K. and the U.S.A., at that time had their own policies. The U.K. thought that it could still retain its influence over the subcontinent by weakening both India and Pakistan; the U.S.A. at that time, I think, was following mainly the British policy in that area because they thought Britain knew best or better than they did. The issue became enlarged and complicated and instead of getting justice from the U.N., the U.N. converted the question of Pakistan's aggression in Kashmir into "the India/Pakistan question," as they called it. Anyway, Nehru accepted the cease-fire which the United Nations proposed on the first of January 1949, although Pakistan had refused to accept it on that day but only agreed four days later on the fifth of January.

He also accepted the truce agreement which was in three parts: the first part was the cease-fire, which was accepted by both India and Pakistan; the second part related to a demand that Pakistan should withdraw all its regular and irregular forces from the occupied areas in Kashmir. This Pakistan never implemented and therefore part three, which related to plebiscite, could not be implemented at all.

This situation has existed so long and Pakistan is, according to us, in illegal and forcible occupation of about thirty-two thousand square miles in Kashmir; yet Nehru in the early fifties offered an agreement for peace, cooperation, friendship, and nonaggression to Pakistan. But the Pakistani leaders, mainly perhaps to bolster their own positions and to rouse the people against India, refused to accept it. It is ironical that Pakistan today is talking of a nonaggression pact with India, yet for thirty years it has not accepted peace, cooperation, friendship, trade and transit. Well, the world has seen many nonaggression pacts which have been treated as scraps of paper. We know about the Molotov/Ribbentrop pact for one. We would very much like to improve relations with Pakistan because we believe that the prosperity and stability of Pakistan are in our own interest.

But you know what happened during the Bangladesh struggle for freedom. Mrs. Gandhi came to the United States in October, 1971. She pleaded with President Nixon to intercede with President Yahya of Pakistan to get Sheikh Mujib, who was the elected leader of Bangladesh, released and have a political settlement with him which would have maintained the integrity of the whole of Pakistan. But President Nixon threw up his hands. He said he couldn't do it or he wouldn't do it. So nothing happened then. Pakistan declared war against India on the morning of the fourth of December, 1971, having the previous evening bombarded nine of our airfields in the west. Well, the result was the breakup of Pakistan, mainly due to their own stupidity because they had maltreated the Bengalis in Bangladesh—treated it as a colony.

On the question of Goa, Mr. Nehru negotiated for fourteen years with the Portuguese government in order to bring about a transfer of Goa to India because it was in the heart of India. The French had agreed to give up their colonies, of Piondichery, Chandernagare and Mabe in the heartland of India, but the Portuguese were stubborn. And again in that year both Britain and the U.S.A.—because Portugal was a NATO partner—tried to frighten us. I happened to be acting commissioner in London at that time and I remember a long conversation with Lord Hume who was the foreign secretary. He said, "You have a strong case on Kashmir. Why did you go to the United Nations?" I said, "It was your representative, Lord Mountbatten, who advised us to do so. You had better ask him." He said, "You have a point there."

Then on Goa, on BBC-TV he said, "We have ordered six warships to sail from the Persian Gulf to Goa to save half a dozen British lives there." I was asked on independent TV, the same evening, "What was your reaction? I said, "Before the six warships arrive there, we will have liberated Goa and the half dozen British lives would be quite safe in our hands."

I am merely mentioning Kashmir, Goa, and Bangladesh to prove that Nehru and his daughter Indira Gandhi tried their best to have a peaceful settlement on all these questions but it was only when he failed, particularly in the case of Goa, that we had to take police action there in order to save our own people and the unarmed people in Goa whom Portugal was gunning down. In any case, we do not think that Portugal had any right over Goa, treating it as a distant colony. India had every right to bring about the peaceful liberation of Goa if possible. I don't have to cite instances in your own history when you have taken over territories that were vital to your security or in the heart of your own continent. Therefore, you should appreciate why we wanted to have Goa with us.

The main change that faces the world today is the threat of a thermo-nuclear war. I sometimes wonder if Mr. Nehru were alive what steps he would take to prevent this mad race of nuclear armaments and the possibility of a nuclear holocaust. I know America says the Soviet Union is superior in some respect, in missiles, and the Soviet Union says America is in others, but these are matters that must be settled through talks and negotiations and not by threatening each other. I think the time has come when no single power of the world can dominate the rest of the world, whether it's America or the Soviet Union, China, India or anybody. And we have willy-nilly, I think, to bring about the *modus vivendi* that will make it possible for different political, social, economic systems to coexist without interfering in one another's internal affairs.

This concept was a contribution of Nehru, namely, the doctrine of Peaceful Coexistence which he had elaborated and which he tried to implement in the formulation of India's relations with other countries. And this is particularly relevant in the thermo-nuclear age of today when war in any corner of the world, if nuclear weapons are used, will spread to the rest of the world and involve the two superpowers as well as other nuclear weapon powers. Nehru's main contribution both as a leader, as prime minister, as foreign minister of India, was to strengthen the process of peace, to weaken the forces of war, to reduce international tensions, and to try to settle international problems peacefully through negotiations rather than through the threat or use of force.

Of course, he didn't succeed in every instance because in foreign affairs you have to deal with foreign governments which are sovereign, which have their own policies, but he did make a very serious effort which bore fruit in many instances. Nehru laid the foundations of a secular, modern, parliamentary democracy in India whose roots have not been shaken in spite of the fact that we have suffered many tremors and shocks and stresses and strains, both internal and external. And Nehru's greatness lies in the fact that he represented not only the hopes and aspirations of the people of India, but I think of the vast majority of humankind for peace and for prevention of war.

I will not presume to compare Nehru's leadership with the leadership you had here. You have a different system, a different society, a different tradition. But there are similarities between Roosevelt and Nehru which I did venture to point out in a seminar we had in Dehli last year on the centenary of President Roosevelt. I won't go into the details, but if you are interested I'll leave a copy of my paper with you.

Also I shall leave a copy of the Nehru Memorial Lecture I delivered in London in December of last year that tries to analyze his role as a leader, as a revolutionary, and idealist.

Question: What is the nature of the disturbances now going on in India? Is it a local affair over autonomy of some sort?

Ambassador Kaul: You are probably referring to the situation in Punjab, the Sikh agitation. Partly it is internal, undoubtedly, because in a large country and a multilingual, multireligious society like we have in India these are problems that were brushed under the carpet during the British rule and they are coming to the surface now that we are independent. Partly they are genuine in the sense that not only the Sikhs in Punjab but people in other states also want greater regional autonomy, provincial autonomy, state autonomy, less control from the center. You'll find these trends even in your country. That is understandable but that's a matter for negotiation.

What's happening in Punjab is that some of the extremist religious fundamentalists, like a man named Bindrawale, for instance, don't want Sikhs to shave their beards. Bindrawale wants pure Sikhism as he conceives it, and he would like, perhaps, to create a kind of Vatican State of the Sikhs in Punjab. He is heavily supported by elements outside India, some Sikhs in this country, and by Pakistanis who are indulging not only in gunrunning but also sending people in disguise. Trying to create disturbances, many Moslems in Pakistan wear turbans, they grow beards, and they pose as Sikhs in the villages. But Mrs. Gandhi tried to settle this through negotiation. She conceded most of the religious demands of the Sikhs, like broadcasting their holy shabad (prayers) from the Golden Temple twice a day. There is Article 25 of the Constitution which most of the Sikhs feel is in their favor so that the advantages given to the lower caste Hindus will be extended to similar castes among the Sikhs. But it is a political struggle, really. The party in power before was the Akali. They could not get a majority themselves so they formed a coalition government. At the last election they lost. They want to come back to power so they are using this extremist religious feeling to come back to power, creating a religious fanaticism so that in the next election they may get more votes.

But as long as it's not a violent movement it's all right. They can do what they like but they will not come around the table and talk with the central government. Perhaps they are afraid of the extremists. My personal opinion is that government will have to take firm action against these extremists. There are not more than three hundred of them but they shoot people and then take shelter inside the Golden Temple or other Sikh temples. And the government is hesitant so far to go inside these temples to flush them out. But I think sooner than later they will have to do it because this is creating its own reactions among the non-Sikhs. There are more Sikhs outside the Punjab than inside Punjab and they are all against this violent agitation. And some of the non-Sikhs outside Punjab and in adjoining states can take their revenge against the Sikhs living there. And the government, I think, has waited too long. They will have to take firm action against these extremist elements. And then I think the reasonable Sikhs, the Akali party and others will be able to come to the negotiating table and talk things out.

Question: You concluded that you thought if Nehru were in power today in India his suggestion would be to negotiate an arms settlement and not threaten the Russians or another power. Right now things seem to be at an impasse; there doesn't seem to be any logical or theoretical or practical way, to go into negotiations. Somebody needs to take initiatives. Either from your view or from, I presume, the view of Mr. Nehru, what would be those initiatives and who would logically take those initiatives?

Ambassador Kaul: Well, we have taken initiative in the U.N., for instance. We proposed (1) that there should be a ban on the use, testing, and further production of nuclear weapons; (2) the existing stockpile should be frozen; (3) a time limit should be laid down, say one year, two years, three years, during which all nuclear weapons of all countries will be destroyed under international supervision and control and safeguards; and (4) that nuclear technology should be available for peaceful purposes to all countries of the world under international safeguards and these safeguards should be applicable both to the nuclear weapon powers and to the non-nuclear weapon powers. These are some of the concrete steps we have suggested.

Then there is the question of first strike or second strike. To my mind if you ban the first strike you indirectly legitimize the second strike. I'm against all strikes. I've been telling the Russians publicly that we must ban any use of nuclear weapons in any contingency because once nuclear weapons are used there can be no limited nuclear war. I think that is a delusion. Once you use nuclear weapons, tactical or strategic, it spreads throughout the world and then there will be a nuclear holocaust.

These are some of the concrete proposals we have made in the U.N. We hope that the two superpowers and other nuclear weapon powers will get together sooner than later to discuss these things and come to some agreement. But there is a spirit of mutual suspicion, of rivalry, of hatred, of dominance. It is not easy to overcome this legacy but it is possible to do so. And the mass campaigns that are going on in western Europe, in Asia, even inside the Soviet Union, and in America, demonstrate that public opinion by and large is against this nuclear armaments race.

Question: Do you feel that the United States or Russia could take an initiative without being at any disadvantage, either one or both of them?

Ambassador Kaul: I think so because they have fourteen times overkill capacity. They could at least reduce it one time kill capacity which is enough to destroy both of them and the whole world. That is the first initiative they can take.

Question: How would you respond, Mr. Ambassador, to the many Indian critics of Mr. Nehru who say that however successful Mr. Nehru may have been on the international arena, however many points he scored for India as a statesman and perhaps as statesman of the world in the late forties and fifties and early sixties, what good has it done India? He may have tried too hard to be a world statesman and not hard enough tending the political and economic and social issues of a very large and complicated and threatening society at home. In other words, what has India to show for all this wonderful statemanship in the United Nations and elsewhere?

Ambassador Kaul: Well, Nehru was responsible for starting a chain of national laboratories. He was responsible for embarking on a huge program of multipurpose dams, something like your TVA, for the generation of electricity, for providing irrigation to the fields and fertilizer factories. He was also responsible on the cultural side for setting up national academies in arts and letters, song, dance, drama which have branches in all the states. He was also responsible for reforming the Hindu civil code by giving the right of divorce and inheritance to women, which was denied before, and for introducing monogamy among the Hindus who previously could have any number of wives. His one weakness was that he was not able to introduce a uniform civil code for all Indian citizens irrespective of religion. I asked him once, "Why don't you also apply the same civil law to the Muslims and non-Hindus?" His reply was, "I believe in democracy. If I applied it to the Muslims, the Muslim fanatic religious leaders will raise a hue and cry and there will be religious revivalism and fanaticism again. So let the opinion spring from within the Muslims themselves and then we shall be able to do it." He even threatened to resign on the question of the Hindu code because the then president Rajendra Prasad, who was an orthodox Hindu in some ways, was against it. Nehru said, "I'll resign, you carry on the government." So he roused public opinion for it among the Hindus and was able to introduce this reform.

On the question of untouchability, he did pass legislation which made it a criminal offense. He raised the marriage age of girls from fourteen to eighteen, of boys from eighteen to twenty-one. Then he was also responsible for introducing land reforms though I must say his colleagues in the various states did not implement them fully. They left loopholes within the land legislation which enabled the big landlord to subdivide his land among his relatives and cousins.

Nehru could have been a benevolent dictator but he was a democrat to the core of his heart. He believed, as he wrote in an anonymous article on himself way back in 1936, "Nehru can be a dictator." He criticized himself. The point is that he had so much faith in the democratic process that although he knew it was a slower process with its loopholes and defects, in the long run he would be able to enlist the cooperation of the vast masses of people through the democratic process rather than otherwise. I once asked him, "Why do you appoint people in positions of authority in key positions who do not believe in your ideology?" He said, "Young man, remember one thing. The Indian people by and large are orthodox, conservative, driven by caste, religion, regional feelings, parochialism. I have to carry the mass of the people with me. It is no use my issuing declarations and giving orders and passing legislation unless I can carry all these people with me. Those who believe in my ideology will always be with me. It's the others, and they are in the majority, whom I have to convert and carry with me." So he suffered fools sometimes because he was a democrat or partly because they had been in British jails with him during the struggle for independence. Perhaps that was a fault, but he was generous as well as democratic to a fault.

Narrator: What do you think of a couple of the American criticisms? One criticism that burned with white heat at the time was of Krishna Menon. He was, as somebody has said, your John Foster Dulles.

Ambassador Kaul: That was probably a correct description, in the circumstances.

Narrator: He was moralistic and that turned some people off. We talked before we came in about some of the private efforts in India. When Dean Rusk was president of the Rockefeller Foundation he asked Mr. Nehru, given the fact that Rockefeller like other foundations had limited resources, which university would Mr. Nehru think would be the university, under a university development program, that an outside group might most appropriately help? Which did he think was the best and most promising one and Mr. Nehru's answer was, "They're all promising." He would never depart from that. That was one reason that things like the All India Medical Institute got support. One could depart from the egalitarianism in that regard.

The third American criticism is one you've heard many times, I'm sure, of a certain hypocrisy on some issues. India did after all in the case of China, the Tibetan crisis, take action. India did arm. India was prepared when its own national interest was threatened to use force. And yet when others turned to force India was, according to this view, the first to criticize and was not always sympathetic with nations that felt they had to use force. What is your reaction to these U.S. criticisms?

Ambassador Kaul: Well, first of all, Krishna Menon was a very clever man and had a very sharp brain; he thought fifty yards ahead of anybody else. But all great men have their defects also; he had a very sharp tongue. I remember an article in *Esquire* magazine where he was described as the "most hated diplomat" in the world. But he had a very tender heart, I can also tell you that. Henry Cabot Lodge, I think, once said, "He was one of my best friends." But as you yourself answered the question, you had your John Foster Dulles and we had our Krishna Menon. All countries have them. But he played a positive role during the Suez crisis and during the Indochina crisis and the Korean war. Don't forget the positive contributions he made. He had a very sharp tongue and he had a knack of converting friends into enemies but not making friends out of enemies. Mr. Nehru tolerated him because he had his uses, but he did not always agree with him. As you remember in 1962 he had to dismiss him as defense minister because public opinion was so strong against Krishna Menon.

The second point you mentioned was about Tibet. In 1950, when China sent its forces into Tibet, we did lodge a protest with the Chinese government. But the Tibetan delegation which had visited London and Washington drew a blank from the British Foreign Office and the State Department. Perhaps they wanted India to take the chestnuts out of the fire and burn our own fingers and we were in no position to do so. We had our trouble with Pakistan at that time. But in spite of that we did lodge protests with the Chinese which they rejected. But in 1954 we accepted Tibet as a part of China in the hope that they would give a large amount of autonomy to the Tibetans which they had promised. Unfortunately, again the Chinese did not play the game but we were in no position to fight China at that time over Tibet. Every country, of course, thinks first and foremost of its own national interests and it is not that we could decide for other countries, if they thought they were protecting their own national interests.

Also, the closer we are to a particular situation, the more we are affected by it. We are less affected by distant problems. Mr. Nehru did criticize both the Soviet Union and the United States. He criticized the Soviet Union in the case of the Hungarian situation and later on the Czech situation when it occurred. He similarly criticized American policy in the Dominican Republic and Guatamala but in very guarded tones. And if you compare the two I think they are almost equally balanced.

I don't know what other instances you have in mind where we have criticized countries which have used force to protect their national interests. We're not against that but we certainly are against a colonial power trying to defend its territories or colonies abroad through the use of force like the Dutch tried to do in Indonesia. Mr. Nehru did call a conference in New Delhi in 1949 against the Dutch aggression in Indonesia and we were able to enlist the sympathy and support of the U.S.A. and some other governments and compelled the Dutch to withdraw from Indonesia.

Narrator: I suppose the Pakistan-India clash, Kashmir, all of these are sometimes mentioned. When the conflict is closer to home you do seem to recognize that force is not excluded.

Ambassador Kaul: Force is the last resort. We have never invaded Pakistan; it is Pakistan that has invaded Kashmir which legally and constitutionally is an integral part of India. In spite of the fact they they used force that started the war we have allowed them to remain in the occupied territory although we could have thrown them out in 1948. You may recall that in 1971 we had occupied five thousand square miles of Pakistani territory in West Pakistan but under the Simla Agreement of 1972 we agreed to vacate it; we gave it back to them. We did not start the war but once you are attacked you've got to defend your country.

Question: With respect to India's educational institutions, there is great virtue in saying you would help every institution equally. But has that kept you from having a Harvard or a Yale or a Virginia?

Ambassador Kaul: Well, we have the Indian institutes of technology. One of them is under Indo-U.S. cooperation in Kanpur; one we have with Soviet cooperation in Pawai, Bombay; there is one in Delhi; there's a fourth one somewhere in Bengal.

Unfortunately, some of the projects had the CIA behind them. I'll name one—the Himalayan Border Countries Project in the sixties. Some American professors who came to me were working on that project when the *New York Times* revealed that the CIA had financed some of these projects and sent their agents as scholars. So the American professors resigned from it and we had to be a little more careful in accepting CIA funded projects in our country. We closed down the American library scheme. We said we would take control of it. If you are prepared to accept our control, we'll run them for you. You can send your scholars but we will not let control remain in the hands of foreigners.

The only positive agreement I was able to achieve as ambassador of India with Henry Kissinger was to set up the Indo-U.S. Commission and its various subcommissions, which I think is doing very good work. We have exchanges of scholars, scientists, professors, students and others. I think the difficulty is, if I may be frank and speak not as a diplomat, that the U.S. is used to dealing either with allies or with client states. They have yet to learn to deal with friends like India. We may not agree but our relationship should be based on equality, reciprocity, and mutual respect. If you try to dominate us we will not accept that. We are a proud people, too; we have an ancient culture and civilization. You are advanced in science and technology, and we admire you for it, but let's have a friendly relationship based on mutual understanding and reciprocity. I think that will endure in the long run rather than the picture of the ugly American or the ugly Indian. We are facing that problem with some of our neighbors, too.

Professor Khare: May we hear something more on the human element of Nehru? We will benefit from listening to anecdotes that reveal other dimensions of his personality.

Ambassador Kaul: Well, I recall when I was ambassador in Moscow we were celebrating Nehru's birthday and there was a seminar like this. The Russian said, "You know, Nehru was a good chap but he was not a scientific Marxist." I said, "He was much more than that; he was a humanist and his humanism transcended both capitalism and communism." They reluctantly had to agree with me. I think the greatest quality of Nehru was his humanism. And I recall, for instance, when talking about science and technology, he said, "They are very important both within a country and to bring about international cooperation. But science and technology should not be allowed to bring down the quality of life. Otherwise life will become dust and ashes."

There was also a letter he wrote to *Shankar's Weekly* about children. He said, "Children play with each other; children may quarrel with each other, and even their quarreling is like play; there is no feeling of class consciousness or class hatred among them." And he added, "The younger generation is better than the older generation in that respect."

His humanism perhaps went too far sometimes as I said. He tolerated fools sometimes, but he was so human that he could not hurt the feelings of others, and he tried to take them along with him to the maximum extent he could. I could give you many anecdotes but this is not the time. There is one I will relate.

During the 1947 riots—the post-partition riots and pre-partition riots, when Hindus and Sikhs were being massacred in what is now Pakistan and Muslims were being massacred in India he personally went with his baton in his hand right into the riot areas. He came across a Sikh with a bundle of new leather shoes on his back. He said, "What are you doing with them?" and he said, "Well, I looted them from the Muslim shop. There's plenty more left, you go in and take some, too." He risked his personal safety but he of course made the man give back the loot.

And particularly during 1947 and 1948 he was the greatest supporter of the Muslim. Some of his colleagues said, "Nehru is the only nationalist Muslim in India," because he favored and supported the Muslims even at the risk of his own life.

Narrator: Is the movie "Gandhi" at all faithful to the Nehru you knew?

Ambassador Kaul: I asked Richard Attenborough about the movie and he said the focus is on Gandhi and therefore it portrays Nehru in a much weaker light. It doesn't bring out his finer qualities. That's why I'm anxious that we should produce at least a documentary about Nehru and his colleagues in the freedom struggle which would give a fairer representation of these leaders. They were very great men, I must say, who made great sacrifices—Nehru more than anybody else. They have not been portrayed properly. But that's a defect because the film is mainly about Gandhi. It portrays Gandhi very well.

Question: Mr. Ambassador, you've spoken about the most important dimension of Nehru's political life as it affected his role as peacemaker and you've done that really in a superb way to illuminate his role in the international arena. You said at the conclusion of your remarks that he had also been concerned with developing a secular democratic parliamentary society in India and that in his humanism he was concerned with enhancing the quality of life of all of us and most particularly, of course, with India and Indians. I'm not going to ask you to comment on his role in facilitating those qualities of life in India as he did in so many ways. You referred to some of them in your response to Professor Barnett's question.

What I would like to do, Mr. Ambassador, is ask you very briefly to turn to the main point of this lecture—the concept of leadership. You've explained that in terms of his role as peacemaker. I ask you, just for a moment, to reflect to us in your experience with the prime minister on that particular question, because when Mr. Nehru was prime minister, as you know so well, in the public press of the world (in some sense India shared this but not nearly so much as the Western press) there was this great anxiety, which as it turns out of course was ill-founded and ill-based, about who would follow Nehru. As it turns out, of course, the institutional fabric of Indian political life quite accommodated to that contingency. But apart from the fact, Mr. Ambassador, the question that I really would like to ask is the question of, not only Nehru's personal leadership, but more particularly his sense of leadership and succession and India's future apart from the institutional strengths of Indian political life that have accommodated so well for that problem. Did Nehru, in your association with him, think about political leadership to follow him?

Ambassador Kaul: I had the temerity to ask him twice. Once in 1956 in the midst of a conference of our ambassadors in New Delhi I sent him a one page note in which I raised among other things this question, "The first line of leadership will soon run out, what about training the second line of leadership?" He read out my note without mentioning my name and answered each and every point. And on this point he said, "In a democracy leaders are thrown up by the democratic process. It's true that the first line of leadership has the halo of the freedom struggle round them which the second line will lack but we are trying to train them up and give them opportunities through the democratic process."

Then again in 1964, two months before his death, I was in Delhi for consultations. I was alone with him. I said, "Shastri is already doing some of your work as minister without portfolio. Why don't you nominate him as your successor?" He smiled and said, "You're right, he is already doing most of my work, but if I nominate him it will not help him. Winston Churchill nominated Anthony Eden as his successor and did more harm than good for Anthony Eden. I don't want that to happen. The party will elect him or anybody else they wish." And I think he proved right.

One point I will say in criticism of Nehru is that he did not devote sufficient attention to the training of the second line of leadership which he could perhaps have done. That criticism I think holds true of all the democratic governments, perhaps not the authoritarian governments who have a second line of leadership, whether good or bad, to fall back upon. But once a democracy becomes stable, I think Nehru's doctrine is correct that the democratic process throws up a natural leader. He may not be the best leader but that is democracy.

Question: Well, we, of course, all suffer those consequences.

Narrator: The Miller Center and I am sure the Committee on the Individual In Society is honored that you would talk about someone with whom you had such close ties. Little by little we try to put together fragments of knowledge about political leaders. Sometimes we are helped by the contemporary discourse but oftentimes we are led astray and you have helped to bring us back to a path where there is a good deal more truth, and we certainly thank you for that.

CONCLUDING OBSERVATIONS

Kenneth W. Thompson

Having listened to or read thoughtful impressions of American presidents and leadership in general from observers abroad, it would be presumptuous to summarize their views. What is appropriate, however, it the suggestion that Americans must seek a deeper understanding of presidential leadership from sources wherever they may be found. The workings of the presidency is not beyond improvement. The insights that can strengthen the conduct of our political system are not bounded by nationality or geography.

The first four essays in the present volume comment directly on the American presidency. The last two papers discuss the context of American leadership in Central and Latin America and the vision of leadership of an inspiring Indian prime minister. Students of American institutions who would exclude such comparative experience from the study of political leadership are shortsighted. At the same time, wise observers from abroad are quick to point out the difficulty of making direct application of comparative knowledge.

The current volume is the second in a series of Tenth Anniversary volumes of the Miller Center with others to follow. Its emphasis on knowledge from other political systems symbolizes the breadth of perspective the Center seeks to encourage. No world class institute in any field can afford to ignore important lessons from other cultures and societies. We intend to continue the effort which we began with a brilliant young Australian professor from Oxford University who was struck down by cancer at the height of his powers.